Making Reading Relevant
The Art of Connecting

Teri Quick
Melissa Zimmer
Diane Hocevar
Metropolitan Community College
Omaha, Nebraska

PEARSON
Prentice
Hall

Upper Saddle River, New Jersey 07458

Library of Congress Cataloging-in-Publication Data

Quick, Teri.
    Making reading relevant : the art of connecting / Teri Quick, Melissa Zimmer, Diane Hocevar.
        p. cm.
    Includes index.
    ISBN 0-13-194406-1
    1. Reading (Higher education)   I. Zimmer, Melissa.   II. Hocevar, Diane.   III. Title.
    LB2395.3.Q53 2007
    428.4071'1--dc22   2006021759

Editorial Director: Leah Jewell
Executive Editor: Craig
  Campanella
Production Liaison: Joanne
  Hakim
Editorial Assistant: Deborah
  Doyle
Director of Marketing: Brandy
  Dawson
Marketing Manager: Kate Mitchell

Marketing Assistant: Kimberly Caldwell
Manufacturing Buyer: Benjamin Smith
Cover Art Director: Jayne Conte
Cover Illustration/Photo: © Getty Images
Permissions Specialist: Lisa Black
Full-Service Project Management:
  Pine Tree Composition
Composition: Laserwords Private Limited
Printer/Binder: RR Donnelley & Sons Company
Cover Printer: RR Donnelley & Sons Company

Credits and acknowledgments borrowed from other sources and reproduced, with permission, in this textbook appear on pages 175–176

Microsoft® and Windows® are registered trademarks of the Microsoft Corporation in the U.S.A and other countries. Screen shots and icons reprinted with permission from the Microsoft Corporation. This book is not sponsored or endorsed by or affiliated with the Microsoft Corporation.

Pearson Education LTD., London
Pearson Education Singapore, Pte. Ltd
Pearson Education, Canada, Ltd
Pearson Education—Japan
Pearson Education Australia PTY,
  Limited

Pearson Education North Asia Ltd
Pearson Educación de Mexico, S.A. de C.V.
Pearson Education Malaysia, Pte. Ltd
Pearson Education, Upper Saddle River, New Jersey

10 9 8 7 6 5 4 3 2 1
ISBN 0-13-194406-1

Contents

Preface   v

Acknowledgments   viii

1 Vocabulary Strategies   **1**
Vocabulary Strategies Overview   3
A. Context Clues   3
   1. Definition   4
   2. Example   5
   3. Contrast   6
   4. Inference   7
B. Word Analysis   10
   1. Syllabication   11
   2. Root Words, Prefixes, Suffixes   12
   3. Latin and Greek   14
C. Denotation and Connotation   21
Quick Connections   24

2 Basic Comprehension Strategies   **25**
Comprehension Strategies Overview   27
A. Identifying Topics   27
B. Identifying Main Ideas   30
C. Identifying Details   35
D. Improving Comprehension   38
Quick Connections   41

3 Textbook Strategies   **43**
Textbook Strategies Overview   45
A. Identifying and Using Textbook Organizational Aids   45
B. Textbook Reading Methods   48
   1. SQ3R   49
   2. 3C   52
   3. Triple Highlighting   54
C. Skimming and Scanning   56
Quick Connections   61

4 Critical Reading Strategies   63

Part A: Critical Reading Strategies Overview   65
A. Predicting, Making Inferences, and Drawing Conclusions   65
   1. Predicting   65
   2. Making Inferences and Drawing Conclusions   69
Part B: Critical Reading Strategies Overview   75
B. Analyzing and Synthesizing   75
   1. Identifying Writer's Purpose   75
   2. Fact and Opinion   76
   3. Judging Validity   78
   4. Identifying Author Attitudes, Bias, Tone, and Assumptions   82
Quick Connections   87

5 Figurative Language Strategies   89

Figurative Language Strategies Overview   91
A. Metaphor and Simile   91
B. Personification   98
C. Hyperbole   100
Quick Connections   104

6 Patterns of Organization Strategies   107

Patterns of Organization Strategies Overview   110
A. Narration   113
B. Description   115
C. Process Analysis   117
D. Classification   120
E. Comparison/Contrast   125
F. Cause and Effect   127
G. Definition   130
Quick Connections   134

7 Graphic Organizer Strategies   137

Graphic Organizer Strategies Overview   140
A. KWL   142
B. Concept Web (or the Five Ws)   145
C. Cause and Effect Chain   146
Quick Connections   152

8 Computer Reading and Writing Strategies   153

Computer Reading and Writing Strategies Overview   155
A. How to Search the Internet   155
B. Evaluating Websites   160
C. Word Processing Basics — A Reference Guide   167
Quick Connections   173

Index   177

Preface

Sometimes less is more. In this age of information overload, it seems imperative that students learn to become better, more efficient readers—and not by reading volumes on *how* to read, but by exposure to essential reading strategies with a major focus on application using "real-life" materials, or primary reading sources.

FEATURES

This text addresses all reading topics necessary for success in college reading, as well as those assessed on state-wide reading tests (including Texas and Florida). It is intended for use in any college reading course, from college prep to higher level, within a variety of contexts:

- Reading courses that incorporate primary reading sources such as newspapers, newsmagazines, novels, textbooks, and the Internet, *or* as a stand-alone text. Essential reading strategies are presented, but the choice of primary sources should be consistent with the reading level of the course.
- Reading courses "paired" or "linked" with a content-area course
  - Students could use the content course textbook as their primary reading source, and would truly be *Making Reading Relevant*.
  - When reading is paired with a writing course, this text helps students see the strong connections between reading and writing. It includes a chapter about patterns of organization, which coincides well with most developmental writing courses. The text offers extended writing practice in the Learning Activities sections of the *Instructor's Manual*.
- Online reading modules or courses
  - Due to the increasing demand for online courses, the text lessons and Learning Activities (included in the *Instructor's Manual*) are structured to be easily adapted for the development of online reading modules.
- Reading courses on a quarter system, because of the brevity of the text
- Reading courses on a semester system, which focus on the *application* of strategies, using primary reading sources.

The text and *Instructor's Manual* are structured to help students (and instructors) work through the lessons *quick*ly and meaningfully. Each text chapter includes the following:

- **Stated objectives** followed by a **readiness quiz**
  - The readiness quiz is not meant to be a true pretest; its purpose is to help gauge the prior knowledge of the students and to serve as a bridge to the chapter.
- Learning **strategies** with featured *QUICK* Tips to highlight some of the more important strategies
- **Practices** using a variety of concise real-life content within the text
- Suggested **learning activities**
  - For extended practice and/or post-testing, the learning activities, as well as the *quick* chapter check-up quizzes in the *Instructor's Manual*, may be used. The IM also includes ideas for teaching the text strategies.

This text is designed to be consumable. For maximum benefit, students need to actively respond to the passages and practices in the book by reading, writing, annotating, and highlighting as needed.

Most reading texts currently available are much longer, more expensive, and require a greater commitment of students' time. We believe that reading courses that stress the use of primary sources are more effective if the bulk of the *in-class practices* use those sources rather than the text. The text could be read outside of class in preparation for classroom practice. The brevity of the text may encourage more (not less) outside reading by today's students, who are often reluctant to read extensively or whose busy lives limit time available for homework assignments.

When introduced to new concepts, students benefit from instruction that connects the learning to the place(s) in their environments (work, school, home) where they can use it. Real-life materials might include chapters from content area textbooks, current event and editorial resources (such as magazines and newspapers), novels, college catalogs, recipes, written directions, and Internet websites. Current brain research indicates that "students are natural learners, are energized by learning, and apparently, love to learn—when they can start learning something new from where they are, using what they already know, and can do their own exploring, thinking, and discovering" (Smilkstein, 2003). This research supports the use of active learning using real-life materials to foster authentic and lasting learning.

For several years, we searched for a simple, concise text to use in our reading classes. We did not find a brief text that addressed all of the topics we wanted to include. Neither did we find anything that stressed the application of reading strategies using primary reading sources as the basis of the content. This text was written to fill those needs.

TO THE STUDENT

How important is reading to you?

As a student, reading serves as a major tool for learning. You probably have discovered that *how well* you read can and will determine the degree of success you achieve in your classes.

Whether you are taking courses in business management, nursing, welding, or any other subject matter area, you will be required to read for information, to follow directions, to understand what you read, and to think critically. Whatever your current reading level, you are taking a positive first step in reaching your academic and career goals by taking a reading course.

Making Reading Relevant: The Art of Connecting will introduce you to a comprehensive set of reading strategies. You can use these strategies as tools for learning in your college courses and for managing reading tasks you will meet on the job and in daily living. The text was designed to minimize the number of practice passages so that you can apply the text strategies to real-life reading materials that are interesting and relevant.

Good reading is an art, much like playing baseball or playing the piano. A teacher can show you how to hold the bat, or how to put your fingers on the keys, but in order for you to hit home runs or become a concert pianist you need to practice. Our hope is that you will read this text, complete the practices, apply the strategies to real-life materials, and go on to be a highly successful student!

Teri Quick
Melissa Zimmer
Diane Hocevar

Acknowledgments

Making Reading Relevant is dedicated to all of our family and friends who offered encouragement and support.

From Teri, special appreciation goes to:
Ted Quick, my husband and constant supporter
Brad and Chet, my sons, who are always a part of me, and Tonia, my daughter from the heart
Tina Peil, my sister, who was always with me through writing the book
Loreen Blakeman, my Mummy and source of unconditional love
Tom Markin, my dad who encouraged me for years to write a book. He died before the book was published, but he knew it was in the works and was so proud of me.

From Melissa, special appreciation goes to:
Scott Zimmer, my husband, a true partner
Kaleb and Chloe, my children, who make my world go round
Janet Riordan, my late mother, whose love for reading forged my path
Jennifer Rumer, my sister, whose belief in me sustains me

From Diane, special appreciation goes to:
Marty Hocevar, my supportive husband, who is happy that I work and that I enjoy my work
Tera, Kelly, and Adam, my three cherished children who think I work too much
Bob Mancuso, my uncle, who encouraged me to become a teacher
Chic and (the late) Josephine Mancuso, my parents who taught me the importance of love

Thanks also to the following people for their roles in making the book happen:
Laura Mann, for encouraging us to write the book
Craig Campanella, our wonderful editor, for his patience and wisdom
Doug Kerr, for his Instructional Skills Workshop model
Jolene Medley, for her extra set of eyes and her writing suggestions
Tammy Payne, for her word-processing assistance

And also thanks to the following reviewers: Barbara Brown, Olive Harvey College; Christina Chapman, Lewis & Clark Community College; Dr. Marta Cronin, Indian River Community College; Judy Davidson, University of Texas, Pan American; Carrie Dorsey, Northern Virginia Community College; Elizabeth Edwards, Rose State College; Sue Hightower, Tallahassee Community College; Danica Hubbard, College of DuPage; Cherise Millsaps, Surry Community College; Debbie Naquin, Northern Virginia Community College; Rick Richards, St. Petersburg College; Heather Severson, Pima Community College; Melinda Schomaker, Georgia Perimeter College; Sharon M. Taylor, Western Wyoming Community College.

Acknowledgments

...

Vocabulary Strategies

Chapter Preview
Vocabulary Strategies Overview

A. Context Clues
   1. Definition
   2. Example
   3. Contrast
   4. Inference

B. Word Analysis
   1. Syllabication
   2. Root Words, Prefixes, and Suffixes
   3. Latin and Greek

C. Denotation and Connotation

Quick-Fucious Say . . .
          Good Vocabulary Take You Far in Life.

Objective

- Student will be able to successfully determine the meaning of words by using context clues, word analysis strategies, and by understanding denotation and connotation.

Readiness Quiz

Section 1: Match the underlined word on the left to the best definition on the right.

1. _____ Because _hyperactive_ children often become distracted, teachers should provide a calm environment.

2. _____ He is _resilient_, not a weak person.

3. _____ That man drives me crazy; he is so _vociferous_! I wish he would be quiet.

4. _____ Queen Elizabeth is the head of England's _monarchy_.

5. _____ Instead of supporting me, he is _averse_ to my position.

A. rule by royalty

B. loud

C. over active

D. opposed

E. able to recover strength

Section 2: Mark each statement below **T** for true or **F** for false.

6. _____ I know how to divide words into syllables.

7. _____ I know what the Latin root **aqu** means.

8. _____ The connotation of a word is its dictionary definition.

9. _____ The suffix comes at the beginning of a word.

10. _____ Each syllable must have a vowel sound in it.

Vocabulary Strategies Overview

Improving your vocabulary is important to your success in college, as well as to your success in life. In college, you need a well-developed vocabulary in order to comprehend and learn information presented in your textbooks and to write papers that will earn high grades. In life you need a good working vocabulary that allows you to succeed in your career and communicate well with others. Vocabulary is associated with educational level and intelligence. Most educated, intelligent people have broad vocabularies, and like it or not, we are often evaluated by our ability to communicate effectively through the use of the oral and written word.

There are two common strategies for finding the meaning of unfamiliar words: context clues and word analysis. This chapter will describe both. A reader can determine the meaning of many words without having to stop to look them up in a dictionary. The use of context clues and word analysis improves reading comprehension and enhances retention of new words because we tend to remember words we figure out for ourselves.

This chapter will also explain the difference between a word's denotative and connotative meanings. It's important to understand how an author uses words to suggest certain meanings or to evoke emotion in the reader. Understanding denotation and connotation will enable you to notice a writer's word choices and more effectively discern what they are meant to convey. Learning and using the strategies in this chapter will get you well on your way to becoming a more capable reader and communicator!

A. Context Clues

Writers sometimes, knowingly, use words that may be unfamiliar to their readers. Therefore, they may use other clarifying words or phrases to help with the understanding of new words. These words or phrases are called **context clues.** If readers are aware that such clues often exist in words or sentences surrounding the unknown words, they can save time and improve comprehension. Context clues enable the reader to make valid guesses about the meanings of many unfamiliar words.

Review the chart below for an explanation and example of each of the four main types of context clues.

Clue	Explanation	Example
Definition	A definition or synonym (word that means the same) is in the sentence with the word.	**Hypochondria is** abnormal anxiety about one's health.
Example	Examples or illustrations that clarify the word's meaning.	He has many **idiosyncrasies, such as** the inability to cross a bridge, holding his feet up across a railroad track, and not letting his food touch on his plate.
Contrast	The word's antonym, or opposite, appears in the sentence.	The bride was **elated** on her wedding day; **however,** her parents were very heavy-hearted.
Inference	You must apply your background knowledge to the information the context offers.	The classroom was **commodious** enough to hold 30 desks, 30 computer stations, an entire technology center for the instructor, and several large bookcases.

Now practice using the four clues.

1. Definition

Sometimes the context in which an unfamiliar word appears contains a definition in the form of a synonym or a longer explanation. A reader needs to look for a stated definition or synonym in the sentence containing an unfamiliar word.

Using the Clue

Read the sentence and circle the definition of the bold printed word.

1. A **stamen** is the pollen-producing male organ of a flower.
2. Mary **commiserated,** or sympathized, with a friend who had lost her job.
3. To **harass** someone means to continuously annoy him.
4. Those born in the United States have **suffrage** (the right to vote).
5. The study of how people think and learn, **cognition,** is a field that attracts many psychologists.

Look for the following to help locate a definition in the sentence containing an unfamiliar word:

Clue words	Refers to, is defined as, means, is
Words in italics	Partitions are *dividers* for rooms.
Words set off by parentheses, dashes, or commas	I have a disorder, vertigo, that leaves you feeling dizzy and confused.
Synonyms	My new neighbor is a sot, or drunkard.

QUICK TIP:

Commas, parentheses and dashes often set off a word from its definition.

2. Example

Writers often use examples to clarify the meaning of unfamiliar words and terms. Examples are vivid illustrations or explanations that define, either by creating familiar images in your mind, or by recalling familiar objects, ideas, or situations.

USING THE CLUE
Read the sentence and answer the questions.

1. To get along with your partner, do your share of **chores,** for example, sweeping, dusting, cleaning the bathroom, doing laundry, and putting the dishes in the dishwasher.

   What are the chores? _____

   What words let you know "here comes the list"? _____

2. Coughing, runny nose, scratchy eyes, red splotches on your skin and sneezing illustrate a few **ailments** that are usually associated with allergies.

   What are the ailments? _____

   Ailments must be _____

3. Some people are **malcontent** because they have such a negative attitude and find fault with everything.

   What two things does a malcontent do? _____

   _____

4. I would not mind being locked up with a **docile** animal (cat, goldfish), but I would mind a **predatory** (lion, tiger) one!

   What are two examples of docile animals? _____

   Docile must mean _____

5. The museum owner was trying to **authenticate** the portrait from the 1800s and the vase from King Henry's collection.

   What two things were the owner trying to authenticate? _____

   _____

   Authenticate must mean _____

3. Contrast

Sometimes the context in which an unfamiliar word or term appears contains an antonym, or opposite word, that helps define the word. Look for words like *but, on the other hand,* or *however* to signal an opposite word from which you can gain meaning for the unfamiliar word.

USING THE CLUE
Read the sentences and define the words.

1. The climate in the Midwest is never **static;** on the contrary, it changes daily.

   Define static _____

2. In Darwin's day, his theory of evolution was **iconoclastic,** but today many people think it is a reasonable theory.

   Define iconoclastic _____

3. Although he was gone an **eon,** when she saw him, it seemed like only yesterday they had parted.

   Define eon _____

4. Everyone was pleased to discover that the bus driver was **circumspect,** unlike his brother the taxi driver, whose driver's license had been revoked for recklessness.

   Define circumspect _____

5. My teacher has been called **altruistic** because he gave up his professional baseball career to serve as a teacher in a village in Africa. On the other hand, he has been called **egocentric** because he constantly boasts about what he does for others.

   Define altruistic _____

   Define egocentric _____

Contrast clue words	however, on the other hand, in contrast, but, yet, unlike, different

4. Inference

An inference is an informed guess based upon what you already know and the information available. Sometimes you have to make a guess about a word based upon prior knowledge combined with the information given.

USING THE CLUE
Read the sentence and answer the questions.

1. The maniac concocted a **diabolic** plan to end the world.

   Define diabolic _____

2. The elementary teacher's **buoyant** manner made the children feel welcome and at ease on the first day of school.

   Define buoyant _____

3. The **deft** hands of the artist created a beautiful portrait of the queen.

   Define deft _____

4. It was an **enigmatic** situation, and, as the detective, I had to work overtime to put the facts together.

   Define enigmatic _____

5. Living alone for years, the man developed strange and **eccentric** habits.

   Define eccentric _____

QUICK TIP:

Read the words and/or sentences around an unfamiliar word to find clues that help you connect meaning to the word.

QUICK TIP:

Look for signal words like *for example* (to illustrate), *however* (to contrast), *means* (to define), and *therefore* (to infer).

USING THE CLUES IN PARAGRAPHS

Use context clues to determine the meaning of each underlined word in the following paragraphs.

Advertising for tobacco products is the most <u>pervasive</u> evidence of company efforts to keep their products in the public eye. Full-page ads in magazines and on billboards portray young, healthy, successful, physically fit people enjoying tobacco products in a variety of circumstances ranging from <u>opulent</u> restaurants and apartments to rafting, boating, and wind surfing.

_____ 1. pervasive

       a. pertinent   b. common   c. perfected

_____ 2. opulent

       a. bizarre   b. cheap   c. expensive

In today's society, all people have the freedom to explore and develop their potential. We each carry with us responsibility to pursue emotional well being. During our lifetime we each will be faced with choices to grow or choices to <u>stagnate</u>. Our emotional growth depends upon our ability to take active roles in its development.

_____ 3. stagnate

      a. commence   b. stand still   c. endure

Addictions <u>evolve</u> gradually, often from very <u>innocuous</u> beginnings. A person who feels unhappy, overwhelmed, threatened, or bored finds a subject or behavior that produces a state of being the person desires, or that <u>suppresses</u> what the person wants to forget. <u>Moderate</u> use of these behaviors, for example, having an occasional drink or partying with friends, does not <u>constitute</u> an addiction. Some people, however, reach a point where they can experience security or pleasure only when they are involved with this object or behavior. Withdrawal of the object produces anxiety and despair. At this point, when the person has lost control and cannot function without the object, he or she is considered addicted.

_____ 4. evolve

      a. develop   b. shrink   c. evade

_____ 5. innocuous

      a. carefully planned   b. harmless   c. mysterious

_____ 6. suppresses

      a. contradicts   b. subdues   c. combines

_____ 7. moderate

      a. reasonable   b. secluded   c. numerous

_____ 8. constitute

      a. contain   b. abolish   c. establish

Key: 1. B,   2. C,   3. B,   4. A,   5. B,   6. B,   7. A,   8. C

How did you do? Were you able to figure out the meaning of the words by using context clues? Being aware of, and looking for context clues to give you word meaning is the first step in building a better vocabulary. The second step, word analysis, will be explained next.

B. Word Analysis

When a reader comes across an unfamiliar word, there are several options available: Skip the word, stop and look it up in a dictionary, reread the paragraph containing the word and use context clues to try to figure it out, or use word analysis to try to find its meaning. You've just learned how to use context clues, and when you combine those strategies with word analysis, you're well on your way to more effective vocabulary building.

What does "use word analysis" mean? Word analysis is done using two processes in combination. The first one, syllabication (breaking the word into syllables and looking for familiar prefixes, root words, and suffixes), may already be a familiar step. The other part of the process, looking for Latin and Greek word parts, may be less familiar. If so, this section will explain how to learn and use common Latin and Greek roots to help analyze and bring meaning to unknown words. The two processes, syllabication and looking for Latin and Greek word parts, can be done at the same time to quickly find meaning for an unfamiliar word.

Consider, for example, the word **immovable.** If you don't know this word, you can start by dividing the prefix, root word, and suffix. Thus you would have the prefix **im,** the root **mov,** and the suffix **able.** Think about what each part means. **Im** is a common prefix meaning "not." The root word **mov** is a Latin root meaning "move." The suffix **able** means exactly what it looks like—able to do whatever comes before it. Put the three meanings together and you have *not move able*—or not able to be moved—which is what immovable means.

Many words don't have a prefix, root, and suffix, and many don't contain a Latin or Greek part. Even so, any word can be broken into syllables, which makes it easier to see if there are prefixes or suffixes, or a Latin or Greek part. If there aren't, dividing words into syllables may help with pronunciation. Since our listening vocabulary is much greater than our reading vocabulary, we recognize many more words by sound than by sight. Thus, if readers can pronounce and hear a word, there's a good chance they will recognize the word and know its meaning.

Let's review some simple strategies for syllabication, and then we'll preview the most common Latin and Greek roots. Using context clues in combination with word analysis strategies enables the reader to quickly determine meaning for many words that are unfamiliar when first encountered. Being able to find meaning for unknown words is a great way to increase vocabulary, which in turn increases comprehension.

1. Syllabication

Syllabication is the process of breaking a word into syllables. So, what's a syllable? A syllable in a word is equal to one beat. If you have a one-syllable word such as cat, you only say one beat—the entire word, **cat.** We don't pronounce our words letter by letter, like c-a-t, but rather by syllables. A two-syllable word has two beats, like **ta-ble;** a three-syllable word is one like **hos-pi-tal.** When you listen to yourself say a word, each separate beat you pronounce is a syllable. As mentioned before, one way to finding meaning for a word you think you don't know when you first see it is to try to say it. If you recognize the word by sound, and often you will, that's the quickest way to find meaning for a word you didn't recognize by sight.

If you're unable to pronounce a word, you need to divide it into syllables. Then you say each syllable, connect it with the next syllable, and so on, until you can roll the sounds together and hear the entire word. This is called "sounding out" a word, and it's a great way to pronounce, and often find meaning for, an unfamiliar word. There are also a few simple rules to help you know where to divide longer words into syllables so that you can pronounce them correctly.

Before you can start applying the rules of syllabication, here are a couple of basic concepts you need to remember.

- Every syllable must contain a **sounded** vowel. It can be a single vowel sound, like e-nough, or one used with consonant sounds (be-gin). You can't have a syllable without a vowel sound.
- There are two kinds of syllables: open and closed. An open syllable ends with a vowel, which is usually long. A closed syllable ends with a consonant, and the vowel in a closed syllable is usually short.

QUICK TIP:

If you don't remember the long and short vowel sounds, ask your instructor to review them. Many college students have forgotten long and short vowel sounds, but you need to know them to be able to pronounce words.

If we use our sample word **begin,** you know that it contains two syllables, **be-gin.** The first syllable, **be-** is an example of an open syllable, and the **e** has the long sound. The second syllable, **gin,** ends with a consonant, so it's a closed syllable, and the **i** has the short sound. Now we're ready for the rules that will help divide a word into syllables.

Syllabication Rules—Apply in Order

P/R/S   Check the word for Prefixes and Suffixes. The first step is to divide between them and the root word (play-ing, il-legal, un-beat-able).

VC/CV   Check for multiple consonants together between vowels. Divide between the consonants (bub-ble, car-toon, fan-tas-tic).

V/CV   If you know the vowel is long, or if there's a single consonant in the middle of a word, divide after the long vowel, or before the single consonant (fa-vor, le-thal, hu-mid).

VC/V   If the vowel before a single consonant is not long, then you divide after the consonant, leaving a closed syllable (hon-ey, drag-on, plur-al).

Here are more points to keep in mind when you're using syllabication:

- Don't divide between consonant digraphs (some examples are *sh, ch, wh, th, str, ck, ng*) because they have one sound and are treated like one consonant (le-thal, noth-ing, buck-le).

- Rarely would you divide between two vowels, because most pairs of vowels only have one sound (rain, teen, loud).

The first step in analyzing an unknown word is to divide it into syllables. The second step is to look at the prefixes, root word, and suffixes to see if you know their meanings.

2. Root Words, Prefixes, Suffixes

Once you've divided a word, look at the first and last syllables to see if they include a common prefix and/or suffix. Prefixes come at the beginning of the word and change or modify the meaning. Suffixes do the same thing, but they're added at the end of a word. Prefixes generally have more meaning than suffixes. Many suffixes are used to change the tense (*ed* or *ing*), or to show the state or condition of the root word (*ar, al*). Other suffixes do carry meaning, such as *able/ible* (able to), or *ful* (full of).

Some of the most common prefixes mean *not,* or the opposite of what the word means without the prefix. You may recognize the ones in the list below:

un	unhappy
in	inadequate
il	illegal
im	immeasurable
ir	irrational
a	asexual

Train yourself to immediately recognize these prefixes and know that they mean *not,* or the opposite of what the word would be without the prefix. Other common prefixes you should immediately register meaning for are *re*—again, *pre*—before, *co* or *con*—together, and number prefixes such as *uni*—one, *bi*—two, and *tri*—three. Studying common Latin and Greek word parts will teach you the meaning of many more prefixes.

The core of a word is the part we call the root. This is the part that has the main meaning. Because many words are made by adding prefixes and suffixes, the root of the word is often in the middle. Most long words are just a root word with several prefixes and suffixes added. That's why breaking words apart can often show you quickly what they mean if you know the meanings of the separate parts. For example, a word like irreplaceable may look long and unfamiliar to you. But if you break it into syllables, starting by dividing off the prefixes and suffixes, you end up with this: ir-re-place-able. Look at each of those parts and substitute the meaning for the prefixes, root and suffix, and you see: not-again-place-able. This is what the word means: not able to place again, or not able to be replaced. Many longer words are just a string of prefixes and suffixes, so separate those from the root word, and you'll see that long words can be easy to pronounce.

QUICK TIP:

Most long words are made up of a root word with added prefixes and suffixes—take words apart to make them easy to define.

Of course, since the root of a word is the basic part with the most meaning, you have to know what the root means to get meaning for an entire word. This is where the Latin and Greek come into the process of word analysis.

3. Latin and Greek

Over half of the English language is based on Latin and/or Greek word parts. Learning some of the most common Latin and Greek parts is a fast way to build a better vocabulary. Once you know the meaning of the parts, you will start recognizing them in unfamiliar words, and you will be able to use your knowledge of the word parts along with the context to figure out meanings of unknown words. The Latin and Greek word parts must be memorized (in your long-term memory) in order for them to permanently help you with your vocabulary.

QUICK TIP:

Flash cards are a great way to memorize the word parts and their meanings. Remember to draw pictures on them!

Following are five lists of the most common and widely used Latin and Greek prefixes and root words. There are 20 prefixes or roots in each list. Think of these lists as your Top 100 vocabulary builders. The prefixes and roots need to be memorized and placed in your long-term memory in order for them to be of benefit to you. We suggest learning 20 words a week for five weeks, reviewing all words weekly as they're learned, and taking a final test over all 100 parts. This process will ensure that you'll remember the meanings when you encounter the roots or prefixes in words. Knowledge of these Latin and Greek parts will make a significant improvement in your vocabulary. Remember that the MRR website is an excellent resource for memorizing and practicing the application of Latin and Greek roots and prefixes.

Latin and Greek Prefixes

Word Part	Meaning	Examples	
1. anti	against	antiaircraft	antiabortion
2. co, com, con	together	coworkers	conjoined
3. contra, counter	against	contradict	counterclockwise
4. ex	out	exit	extract
5. hyper	excessive	hyperactive	hyperventilate
6. hypo	under, less	hypodermic	hypothyroid
7. inter	between	interrupt	interstate
8. intro, intra	within	introspective	intramural
9. mis	wrong	misspell	mislead
10. multi	many	multiplication	multilingual
11. peri	around	perimeter	periscope
12. post	after	posttest	postoperative
13. pre	before	prenatal	pretest
14. re	again	redecorate	retake
15. retro	back	retro fashions	retrorockets
16. sub	under	subway	submarine
17. super	above	superintendent	superman
18. syn, sym	together	symphony	synchronize
19. tele	far	television	telescope
20. trans	across	transcontinental	transportation

Latin and Greek Number and Negative Prefixes

Word Part	Meaning	Examples	
1. uni	one	uniform	unisex
2. mono	one	monopoly	monolog
3. bi	two	bisexual	bicycle
4. tri	three	tripod	tricycle
5. quadr	four	quadruplets	quadrangle
6. quint	five	quintet	quintuplets
7. penta	five	pentagon	pentameter
8. hex	six	hexagon	hexagram
9. oct	eight	octopus	octagon
10. dec	ten	decade	decimal
11. cent	hundred	century	centipede
12. kilo	thousand	kilometer	kilogram
13. semi	half	semiconscious	semester
14. un	not	unhappy	unconscious
15. in	not	incapable	incomplete
16. im	not	impossible	immovable
17. il	not	illegal	illiterate
18. ir	not	irregular	irrational
19. a	not	asexual	atypical
20. dis	not	discontent	disable

Latin and Greek Roots

Word Part	Meaning	Examples	
1. am, amat	love	amative	amorous
2. ann, enn	year	annual	anniversary
3. aqu	water	aquarium	aquaplane
4. astr	star	astronomy	astrology
5. aud, audit	hear	auditory	audition
6. auto	self	automatic	autobiography
7. bibli	book	bibliography	Bible
8. bio	life	biology	biography
9. capit	head	capital	decapitate
10. chron	time	chronological	chronic
11. cred, credit	believe, trust	credibility	credentials
12. cycle	circle, wheel	cycle	bicycle
13. dem	people	democracy	demographics
14. derm	skin	epidermis	dermatologist
15. dict	say	dictate	diction
16. dyn	power	dynamite	dynasty
17. fid	faith	confidence	fidelity
18. frater	brother	fraternity	fraternal
19. gram, graph	write	autograph	telegram
20. greg	flock	congregation	gregarious

Latin and Greek Roots

Word Part	Meaning	Examples	
1. hetero	other	heterosexual	heterogeneous
2. homo	same	homosexual	homonym
3. hydr	water	hydrant	hydroplane
4. loc	place	location	locale
5. log	word, study	biology	apology
6. mal	bad	malnutrition	malpractice
7. man	hand	manual	manicure
8. mater, matr	mother	maternity	maternal
9. metr, meter	measure	thermometer	speedometer
10. mit, miss	send	transmit	missionary
11. mor, mort	death	mortuary	mortality
12. mov, mot, mob	move	motion	mobility
13. pater, patr	father	paternity	patriarch
14. ped	foot	pedestrian	pedicure
15. phil	loving	philosophy	philanthropist
16. phon	sound	phonics	telephone
17. prim	first	primary	primitive
18. psych	mind	psychology	psychiatrist
19. pyr	fire	pyromaniac	pyrotechnics
20. reg	rule	regulations	regulate

Latin and Greek Roots

Word Part	Meaning	Examples	
1. rupt	break	rupture	interrupt
2. scrib, script	write	scripture	inscribe
3. seg, sect	cut	section	bisect
4. sol	alone	solo	solitaire
5. soph	wisdom	sophisticated	sophomore (wise moron)
6. spect	look	spectator	spectacle
7. tard	late	tardy	retarded
8. tempor	time	temporary	tempo
9. the	God	theology	atheist
10. therm	heat	thermometer	thermostat
11. tract	pull	tractor	extract
12. turb	whirl, agitate	disturbance	turbulence
13. urb	city	urban	suburb
14. vac	empty	vacant	vacuum
15. vers, vert	turn	reverse	convert
16. vid, vis	see	vision	video
17. vit, viv	life	vital	vivacious
18. voc, vocat	call	vocal	vocation
19. xeno	stranger	xenophobia	xenobiotic
20. zoo	animal	zoology	zoologist

Once you've memorized the Latin and Greek word parts, you need to be able to apply that knowledge by determining meaning for words containing Latin and Greek parts when you see them in sentences. Let's see how that works. Below are 10 sentences containing a word based on Latin or Greek. Refer to the lists (if needed) and determine the meaning of the words in italics. Then indicate whether each sentence is True (**T**) or False (**F**).

_____   1. *Postoperative* procedures occur before an operation.

_____   2. An *intravenous* needle goes within the vein.

_____   3. A *decade* lasts twenty years.

_____   4. An *illiterate* person is a good reader.

_____   5. Your *audio* system needs a big screen for maximum effect.

_____   6. *Demographics* show statistics about people.

_____   7. A *hydroplane* needs a paved landing strip at least 200 yards long.

_____   8. A *biped* has two feet.

_____   9. An *urbanite* lives in a small town.

_____   10. A *soliloquy* is a speech by one person.

By combining the knowledge of word parts with the context of the sentence, you can see how it's possible to determine meaning. Often you don't need to know the exact meaning of unfamiliar words, but if you get a general meaning, it's enough for comprehension. Let's see how you did. Here are the answers:

1. F,   2. T,   3. F,   4. F,   5. F,   6. T,   7. F,   8. T,
9. F,   10. T

Your instructor may give you more application quizzes that will increase your ability to determine meaning by using context clues, syllabication and Latin and Greek word parts. In addition to using these strategies, there's another vocabulary concept you should find helpful. It's described next.

C. Denotation and Connotation

There is a difference between how a word is defined in a dictionary—its *denotation*—and what a word may suggest or how it makes the reader feel. The suggested meaning of a word is called the *connotation*, and this meaning is not found in a dictionary. Connotations are learned as we hear words spoken, or as we read how they're used, in context. Connotation may also result from cultural differences, or how words are used in particular cultures.

Due to connotative meanings, many words create a positive or negative reaction in the reader. For example, one dictionary definition of the verb *travel* is "to go from one place to another" (*Webster's New World Dictionary*, 1995). This word and its meaning are neutral in the sentence below, not really evoking a positive or negative response:

He traveled *all summer*.

However, if a writer wanted to create a more positive image, she might say:

He toured *all summer*.

And if she wanted to communicate a more negative image, she could state it this way:

He drifted *all summer*.

It's important for readers to notice a writer's word choices to more fully understand what the writer is trying to convey.

See if you can identify the more positive connotation in each of the following word pairs.

1. smirk   smile
2. aroma   odor
3. lady   female
4. cram   study
5. desire   lust

The more positive words above are: *smile*, *aroma*, *lady*, *study*, and *desire*. For more practice on positive and negative words, see Chapter Four, Critical Reading Strategies.

You often hear that the best way to improve your vocabulary is to read, read, read, and this is true! But doing all that reading takes time, and as a college student, your time is limited. The strategies we've included in this chapter are shortcuts that can help you increase your vocabulary quickly. Here are a few other tips to help in your quest for a better vocabulary:

- Buy a good college-edition dictionary to use when other strategies aren't enough.
- Buy a thesaurus to supplement your dictionary, particularly when writing.
- Use mnemonics (memory tricks) to help memorize word meanings.
- Make flash cards with pictures to help memorize word meanings.
- Keep a vocabulary notebook to record unfamiliar words, meanings, and sentences containing the words.
- Use new words as much as possible. Use it or lose it!

CHAPTER SUMMARY

- **VOCABULARY STRATEGIES OVERVIEW:** An educated vocabulary is important to academic, career, and life success. There are several strategies that enable a reader to quickly determine the meaning of unfamiliar words.
- **CONTEXT CLUES**
  - **Definition:** Look for a definition or synonym that is directly stated in the sentence containing the unknown word.
  - **Example:** An example or examples of the word are given; these enable the reader to understand the unknown word.
  - **Contrast:** Also called opposite—there's a word in the sentence that means the opposite of the unknown word. If you know the opposite word, you can figure out the unfamiliar word.
  - **Inference:** Use background knowledge, common sense, and the way the unknown word is used in the sentence to figure out meaning.
- **WORD ANALYSIS**
  - **Syllabication:** Knowing how to divide words into syllables enables a reader to sound out and pronounce words to gain meaning from what seems to be an unknown word. Dividing a word

into syllables also shows the reader any prefixes, roots, and suffixes that give meaning.

- **Root words, prefixes, and suffixes:** Over half the English language comes from Latin and Greek. Knowing the meaning of common Latin and Greek word parts is a quick way to expand vocabulary by giving meaning to unknown words containing those parts.

- **DENOTATION AND CONNOTATION**
  - **Denotation:** the dictionary definition of a word.
  - **Connotation:** the suggested meaning of a word.

QUICK CONNECTIONS—CHAPTER ONE

News Source Connection

Choose an article in a newspaper or news magazine to read. As you read, highlight the words you don't know and write each unfamiliar word on a 3 × 5 card. Using the article context for each word, guess the meaning, and write your guess at the top of the other side of the card. After you finish reading the article, look up the definitions of your words and write the correct meanings under the meanings you guessed. If your guessed meaning is correct, you don't need to write it again; just write "correct" and congratulate yourself for using your context clues well!

Textbook Connection

Take a textbook from another class and determine where the vocabulary definitions are located. Are they in a glossary? In the margins? At the beginning or end of each chapter? Make a list of each of your textbooks and where the vocabulary is located. If there is no vocabulary help, note that you need to keep a dictionary handy while reading that text.

Novel Connection

As you survey or preview a course novel, notice unfamiliar words, and make a list of them. Use word analysis (syllabication and pronunciation; Latin and Greek parts) to figure out as many of the meanings as possible. Then look up the meanings in a dictionary, and write the definitions next to the words before you begin reading the novel. You will have created a glossary to go along with your novel!

Computer Connection

Find and bookmark to your personal computer(s) a good dictionary website. Use it often!

Basic Comprehension Strategies

Chapter Preview

Comprehension Strategies Overview

A. Identifying Topics

B. Identifying Main Ideas

C. Identifying Details

D. Improving Comprehension

Comprehension equals understanding . . .
Understanding Equals Learning.

Objective

- Student will be able to comprehend a reading selection by identifying topics, main ideas, and major details; and by knowing strategies to use when confronted with comprehension problems.

Readiness Quiz

Choose **T** for true or **F** for false after reading each statement below.

1. _____ Topic and main idea are the same thing.

2. _____ A topic can be stated in a word or two.

3. _____ The main idea tells the point of the entire passage.

4. _____ All of the details are equally important.

5. _____ There may be a main idea for each paragraph as well as for the entire passage.

6. _____ The topic contains supporting details.

7. _____ The main idea may be stated, or you might have to figure it out.

8. _____ I know what the 5 Ws and H are.

9. _____ The topic is longer than the main idea.

10. _____ I know what to do if I'm having trouble comprehending while reading.

Comprehension Strategies Overview

Comprehension, or understanding, is the ultimate goal of any reader. If a reader doesn't understand what is read, there is no point in reading. Many students say that comprehension is their biggest reading problem. This chapter shows the reader how to break comprehension down into four easy strategies. The first three strategies—being able to identify topics, main ideas and details—are the key elements of comprehension. This text offers a fourth strategy for improving comprehension—a comprehension strategies chart that shows what a reader can do to remedy specific comprehension problems. Readers who can identify the three key elements of comprehension and who also have a reference chart to address specific comprehension problems should experience excellent comprehension.

A. Identifying Topics

In order to comprehend the meaning of what they are reading, readers must first be able to identify three key elements: the topic, the main idea, and the details. The first of these, the topic, is the most basic of the three—the subject of the entire reading. Who or what is the reading about? The topic is very general and can usually be stated in a word or two. If a reader is unable to identify the topic, he or she will not be able to comprehend the reading. This lesson focuses on strategies for identifying the topic as the first step to the comprehension of any reading.

Consider the following paragraph:

> *The cool-down period is an important part of an exercise workout. The cooldown involves reducing the intensity of exercise to allow the body to recover from the workout. During vigorous exercise such as jogging, a lot of blood is pumped to the legs, and there may not be enough to supply the heart and brain. Failure to cool down properly may result in dizziness, fainting, and in rare instances, a heart attack. By gradually reducing the level of physical activity during a cooldown period, blood flow is directed back to the heart and brain.*

What did you just read about? That's the topic of this paragraph. Remember, it's who or what the entire paragraph is about. Did you come up with the topic "cool-down period"? If so, you're right!

Force yourself to state what you've read about (the entire reading) in a word or two. This is the topic.

Let's look at another paragraph to see if you can detect an easy way to identify the topic.

> *One big difference between high school and college is the amount of studying needed. In high school, most students spend very little time studying outside of class or study hall. But in college, much more studying is required. They say to be a successful college student, you should plan to spend two hours studying outside of class for every hour you spend in class. Many new college students have a difficult time learning to spend enough time studying.*

What is this paragraph about? Did you say "studying"? That's correct, but how did you know? Often the word that expresses the topic will be repeated frequently throughout the paragraph or reading. If you see the same word many times, this is a good clue that the repeated word is the topic.

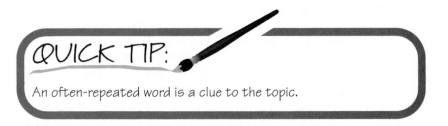

An often-repeated word is a clue to the topic.

Let's see how good you are at identifying topics in paragraphs. Read the following paragraphs and then state the topic on the line below each one. Remember—it should only take a word or two to state what the paragraph is all about!

TOPIC PRACTICE ONE

1. *You may be surprised to learn that the device we call a lie detector does not actually detect lies (Vrij, 2000). What we call*

a lie detector is really a polygraph (literally, "many writings"), an electronic device that simultaneously senses and makes records of several physiological indices, including blood pressure, heart rate, respiration, and galvanic skin response (GSR)—changes in the skin's ability to conduct electrical current that are associated with levels of perspiration. Computerized scoring systems have been developed for interpreting the results (Olsen et al., 1997).

TOPIC _____

2. *School resource officers can benefit law enforcement, school districts, and the community in general. By having the officers in the schools every day, they can open lines of communication between school officials and the law enforcement community. Many times officers and school officials work on the same problems and have to handle the same "bad" kids, but are not able to work closely together for various reasons. The school resource officers help break down these barriers. (Oliver, 2001)*

TOPIC _____

3. *Whether you are a student, an instructor, a prospective author, or a bookseller, this site is the place to find a host of solutions to today's classroom challenges—ranging from traditional textbooks and supplements to CD-ROMs, Companion Websites, and extensive distance learning offerings. (Prentice Hall website)*

TOPIC _____

4. *Few economists doubt that current Bush tax cuts, $290 billion in this year alone, helped stimulate the economy at first. Those rebate checks that arrived in the fall of 2001 helped prop up the economy during a dark period, and consumer spending helped the United States make its way to recovery. Now that the economy is improving, the calculus for tax cuts is different. Will cutting taxes further make a meaningful difference to the economy? And even if it does, can we afford to increase the deficit for the sake of tax relief? (Thottam, 2004)*

TOPIC _____

Now that you've practiced identifying the topic of a paragraph, do you have any questions about it? If you do, write your questions here to ask your instructor.

Next, let's see if you can identify the topic of a longer passage. Read the following passage and then write the topic on the line at the end.

TOPIC PRACTICE TWO

> *In a Californian coastal idyll known for harboring creative types like Ansel Adams, Jack London and onetime mayor Clint East-wood, the latest public nuisance is also the city's very soul—art. With 120 art galleries in a town of 4,058 people, or one gallery for every 34 residents, the city council of Carmel-by-the-Sea voted last month to limit the number of new galleries moving into town. Carmel's leaders decided that the city, which earns no sales-tax revenue when out-of-state tourists snap up a watercolor, has reached aesthetic overkill.*
>
> *Carmel's artistic community is canvas-shredding mad. "The art galleries bring a lot of people to town. They are going to kill the goose that lays the golden egg," says Linda Miller, who runs a gallery with her husband Jim, a painter, on Ocean Av-enue, the city's main drag. Mayor Sue McCloud is unmoved. "We need a more diverse economy," she says.*
>
> *In the past, Carmel has preserved its bohemian charm through ordinances banning streetlights, neon signs and, at one stage, ice cream cones (Eastwood reversed that one in 1986). But the 1-sq.-mi. city has become a victim of its own success, as three-bedroom houses sell for $2 million and the high rents that gallery owners are willing to pay force out mom-and-pop stores. Old-timers shrug at the city's latest dirigiste maneuver. "This is still paradise," says Wilda Northrop of the Carmel Art Assoication. "No matter what happens on Ocean Avenue, there's always the beautiful ocean at the end of the street." (McCarthy, 2004)*

TOPIC _____

Remember—identifying the topic is the first step toward understanding, or comprehending, what you're reading. You have to know what you're reading about. Then you're ready to go on to the second step of comprehension, identifying the main idea.

B. Identifying Main Ideas

The term main idea has different meanings according to different instructors, and is often confused with the term topic. The topic, as you now have learned, is the general subject of the reading. The main idea, on the other hand, is **the point** the reading makes about the topic. The main idea of a passage or reading is the central thought or message. An easy way to understand the difference between main idea and topic is to imagine overhearing a conversation in which you hear your name mentioned often. You know the *topic* of the conversation is you, but you want to know what is being said about you. You probably wouldn't be satisfied until you knew the point they were making about you, or the *main idea*. The same principle applies to reading. The topic is not enough—you also need to know the main idea.

The topic can usually be stated in a word or two, while it takes a sentence to state the main idea. Whether you're reading a paragraph or a longer passage, you will often find one sentence that best summarizes the entire paragraph or passage. This is your main idea statement, which is called a "topic sentence" in a paragraph, or a "thesis statement" if one sentence states the main idea of a longer passage. Since the topic sentence or thesis statement is most often stated toward the beginning of a paragraph or longer reading, look at the first few sentences to see if one seems to be a general statement that makes a point.

QUICK TIP:

Topic = General subject (one or two words)
Main idea = Point made about the topic
Topic sentence = Main idea sentence in a paragraph
Thesis statement = Main idea sentence in a longer passage

Reread the paragraph below in which you identified the topic as being "cool-down period." As you read it now, see if you recognize a sentence that states the main idea of the entire paragraph. Remember, this sentence will tell you what point the writer is making about the cool-down period. What does the writer want you to know about the cool-down period once you've finished reading the paragraph?

> The cool-down period is an important part of an exercise workout. The cool-down involves reducing the intensity of exercise to allow the body to recover from the workout. During vigorous exercise such as jogging, a lot of blood is pumped

to the legs, and there may not be enough to supply the heart and brain. Failure to cool down properly may result in dizziness, fainting, and in rare instances, a heart attack. By gradually reducing the level of physical activity during a cool-down period, blood flow is directed back to the heart and brain.

Did you find the topic sentence, or main idea? It's the first sentence, which tells you that the cool-down period is an important part of a workout. The paragraph then goes on to explain why the cool-down period is important. But what you need to remember is that the cool-down period is important.

Another easy way to locate the main idea is to use the SQ3R textbook study method, which is discussed in the next chapter. One of the many benefits of using this method is that it often points you to the main idea. When using SQ3R, you form questions from each heading, and often the answer to your question will be the main idea for that section.

Let's say that there was a heading in your textbook above the paragraph you just read that said **Cool-down Period.** If you were using SQ3R, you'd make a question from that heading. Since most people know what a cool-down period is, the question you might make from that heading would be something like, "What about the cool-down period?" Then the first sentence would tell you what you need to know about the cool-down period—that it's important.

QUICK TIP:

The sentence that answers your SQ3R question is often the main idea sentence.

If you can't find a sentence that summarizes the point being made about the topic, the main idea may only be suggested, or implied. In that case, **you** need to determine what the main idea is. If there is no stated main idea, determine your own by asking yourself these three questions:

1. What is the topic?
2. What are the details trying to show?
3. What is the **ONE** point being made about the topic?

The answer to question 3 is the main idea.

Read the following paragraph and see if you can determine the point, or the main idea, that the writer is making.

> A news story in Washington, D.C. reports that, of 184 persons convicted of illegal gun possession in a six-month period, only 14 received a jail sentence. Forty-six other cases involved persons who had previously been convicted of a felony or possession of a gun. Although the maximum penalty for such repeaters in the District of Columbia is ten years in prison, half of these were not jailed at all. A study last year revealed that in New York City, which has about the most prohibitive gun legislation in the country, only one of six people convicted of crimes involving weapons went to jail.
>
> (Goldwater, 1975)

Using our three-question method,

1. What is the topic of the paragraph? If you determined that it's about illegal gun possession, you're right.

2. What are the details trying to show? Did you get the idea that people convicted of illegal gun possession aren't punished very often? Each of the examples used pointed out the lack of punishment for those convicted of illegal gun possession.

3. What is the **ONE** point being made about the topic (illegal gun possession)? If you concluded that laws against illegal gun possession in the U.S. aren't being enforced, give yourself an A+!

That's the point, or main idea, that Barry Goldwater was trying to make. He used examples to give details, but he never stated his main idea. It was up to you, the reader, to use your skills to determine the point the writer wanted you to know.

When the main idea is not stated by the writer in a topic sentence, your work as a reader is more difficult; you still need to identify the main idea in order to comprehend what you're reading. When you have to figure out the main idea for yourself because the writer has *implied* it, rather than directly stated it, remember that it's up to you to identify the topic, add up the details, and decide what point the writer is making. In addition to using information stated in the reading, you are also expected to use any background information you already know about the topic to help determine the main idea. Once you've done that, if you're reading from material you can write on, it's a good idea to write the main point in the margin. This will help you solidify the main idea in your mind, and it will help you when you review the material at a later date.

If you're not sure you've found the topic sentence, or that you've made the correct assumption about the main idea, here's an easy way to check yourself. If most of the details are related to the topic sentence you chose, or if they add up to the main idea you stated in your own words, then you're probably correct.

QUICK TIP:

Most of the sentences in the reading should relate to the main idea. If they don't, you haven't found the correct main idea.

Let's try determining the main idea in paragraphs where there is no topic sentence. Read each of the following paragraphs. Using the details given, plus your background knowledge, determine the main idea for each paragraph and write it on the line below the paragraph. The first paragraph is taken from a dental radiography text, and the second is from a psychology text.

MAIN IDEA PRACTICE ONE

Dental Radiography

The operator should always wear protective eyewear, mask, utility gloves, and a plastic or rubber apron when cleaning the tank or changing the solutions. The tank and its inserts should be scrubbed each time the solutions are changed. A solution made up of 1.5 oz (45 ml) of commercial hydrochloric acid, 1 qt (0.95 L) of cold water, and 3 qt (2.85 L) of warm water is sufficient to remove the deposits that frequently form on the walls of 1 gal (3.8 L) inserts. Commercial solutions for cleaning are available. (Johnson, McNally & Essay, 2003.)

MAIN IDEA: _____

Psychology

For nearly a century, researchers have agreed with the proposal that we are sensitive to at least four primary tastes: sweet, sour, bitter, and salty (Henning, 1916; Scott and Plata-Salaman, 1991). Hence it is reasonable to suppose that there are at least four different types (shapes) of receptor sites. The arrangement is like a key fitting into a lock. In this case, the key is the molecule and the lock is the receptor site. Once the sites are occupied, depolarization occurs and information is transmitted through the gustatory nerve to the brain. . . . A number of molecules can occupy a receptor site: The better the fit, the greater the depolarization (McLaughlin & Margolskee, 1994). Keep in mind, however, that the lock-and-key theory is not absolute. Even though a receptor signals a certain taste more than others, it can also contribute to the perception of other tastes (Erickson, DiLorenzo, & Woodbury, 1994).

MAIN IDEA: _____

Whether the main idea is stated in a topic sentence, or merely implied, being able to find the main idea in what you read is **crucial** to your comprehension. If you don't know what the writer wants you to know when you're finished reading, you haven't *really* read the material because *reading is comprehension*.

Now that you know how to identify the topic and the main idea, you're two-thirds of the way to good comprehension. Knowing what the reading is about and knowing the main point the author is making are obviously important to comprehension. But you still need more information to comprehend fully, or understand, everything you need to know. The information that gives you complete understanding is contained in the details—the third element key to comprehension.

C. Identifying Details

Once a reader has identified the topic and main idea of a reading, the next step to comprehension is to find the details that will fill in and complete your understanding. Most readings have many details; some need to be remembered, others don't. The details that relate directly to the main idea are called major details; these are important and need to be highlighted or recorded in some way. Major details explain, develop, support, and give examples of the main idea.

A skilled reader starts to identify the major details by using the 5 W and H questions with the main idea. These questions ask *who, what, when, where, why,* or *how.*

Consider the following paragraph.

Forty percent of children say the American Dream is beyond their reach. A quarter don't feel safe walking alone on the streets of their own neighborhoods. Almost a third of kids under 17 went without health insurance during the last year. Marguerite Sallee, 58, a blond Republican in a power suit, cites these figures to show one thing: America needs to do a better job of caring for its children.

Newsweek magazine, October 3, 2005

To comprehend a paragraph, start by identifying the topic. Here, if you came up with "children," you're right. Next, ask yourself what point is being made about the topic, and whether there is a sentence that states it. The last sentence nicely states the writer's main idea. Now you need your major details to complete your comprehension of this paragraph.

Let's try the 5 Ws and H.

Who? <u>Marguerite Sallee.</u>
What? <u>More caring for children.</u>
When? <u>Now (implied).</u>
Where? <u>America.</u>
Why? <u>Examples: American Dream beyond reach, don't feel safe, no health insurance.</u> How? <u>Not stated in the paragraph, but you would expect the answer in following paragraphs.</u>

With this information, your comprehension of the paragraph should be complete, and you understand what the writer wants you to know.

> ## QUICK TIP:
>
> Start identifying major details by finding the answers to your 5 W and H questions.

After you've identified the most important details by answering your 5 W and H questions, there's another way to find major details if you're reading from a source with headings, and using SQ3R. Find the answers for your SQ3R questions if they're different from your 5 W and H questions. The answers to SQ3R questions made from headings may also be major details. The last step is to look for details that directly relate to or support your main idea. If the detail doesn't tie in directly, it's not a major detail.

QUICK TIP:

Check a detail against the main idea statement to see if it's a major detail.

There are other details that could be left out and the main idea would still be clear. These are called minor details. These details explain a major detail. The minor details are used to add interest, but usually don't need to be remembered, and aren't necessary for comprehension.

To illustrate the difference between major and minor details, read the following paragraph and identify topic, main idea, and the major and minor details.

DETAILS PRACTICE ONE

There are a number of ways to get rid of hiccups. The first way, which many people try, is holding their breath and counting to ten. However, most people never make it to ten because the hiccups take over and interrupt the process. Another common method is to try breathing into a paper bag. I had a friend who tried this and it only made his stomach hurt and his hiccups get worse. Finally, there's the method of trying to scare the hiccups away. If you can get someone to sneak up on you and yell, that might make the hiccups stop. Hopefully one of these methods will work for you.

TOPIC: _____

MAIN IDEA: _____

Major Details	**Minor Details**
1. _____	1. _____
2. _____	2. _____
3. _____	3. _____

How did you do? Was it easy for you to see that the paragraph was telling you about three ways to try to get rid of the hiccups? That's what was important. Knowing that most people can't make it to ten when counting, or what happened to the friend, aren't what you need to know or remember from the paragraph. What you need to know to comprehend the paragraph are the major details, or the three ways to get rid of hiccups. Being able to identify the major details that support the main idea is the final piece to the comprehension puzzle.

Now that you've learned the three key strategies for comprehending your reading materials, you should be well on your way to good comprehension! Knowing how to identify the topic, main idea, and major details in your reading material leads to good comprehension. However, there still might be times when you find yourself losing attention and having difficulty understanding what you're reading. The last comprehension strategy addresses what you should do if this occurs.

D. Improving Comprehension

The following checklist is a great tool for improving comprehension that goes beyond being able to identify topic, main idea, and major details. Sometimes you will find yourself having difficulty comprehending a certain reading and becoming frustrated. That's the time to turn to the Comprehension Strategies checklist. It can help you determine why you're having problems, and how to correct them. To use the checklist, read through the possible problems on the left side. Once you've decided what your problem is, read through the suggestions on the right side and try them until you find a solution that works for you.

NOW REINFORCE THESE COMPREHENSION STRATEGIES BY PRACTICING THEM USING YOUR PRIMARY SOURCES!

Comprehension Strategies

Problems	Strategies
Having difficulty concentrating	1. Take frequent breaks. 2. Read difficult material when your mind is fresh and alert. 3. Use guide questions (see SQ3R). 4. Stop and write down distracting thoughts. 5. Move to a quieter place. 6. Stand or walk while reading.
Words are difficult or unfamiliar	1. Use context clues. 2. Analyze word parts—look for Latin or Greek roots that will give meaning for the word. 3. Skim through material before reading. Mark and look up meanings of difficult words. Jot meanings in the margin or on 3 × 5 cards. 4. Use glossary or margin definitions if available.
Sentences are long or confusing	1. Read aloud. 2. Express each sentence in your own words. 3. Look for key words—subject and verb. 4. Break long sentences into shorter sections.
Ideas are hard to understand; complicated	1. Rephrase or explain each in your own words. 2. Make notes. 3. Locate a more basic text or video that explains ideas in simpler form. 4. Study with a classmate, discuss difficult ideas. 5. Search the Internet for simple explanations of the ideas presented in the text.

(*cont.*)

Problems	*Strategies*

Ideas are new and unfamiliar; you have little or no knowledge about the topic and the writer assumes you do	1. Make sure you didn't miss or skip introductory information.
	2. Get background information by:
	   a. Referring to an earlier section or chapter in the book
	   b. Referring to an encyclopedia
	   c. Referring to a more basic text
	   d. Referring to the Internet

The material seems disorganized or poorly organized or there seems to be no organization	1. Read the Table of Contents— it's an outline of the book and each chapter. 2. Pay more attention to headings. 3. Read the summary, if available. 4. Try to discover organization by outlining or drawing a concept map as you read.
You don't know what is important; everything seems important	1. Use surveying or previewing. 2. Ask and answer guide (SQ3R) questions. 3. Locate and underline topic sentences.

CHAPTER SUMMARY

- **TOPIC:** General subject of passage; can be stated in a word or two.
- **MAIN IDEA:** Point being made about the topic; stated in a sentence.
- **DETAILS:** Two kinds: major and minor. Major details support the main idea and are important. Minor details are less important and usually don't need to be remembered. Use the 5 Ws and H to find the major details.
- **IMPROVING COMPREHENSION:** Use the "Comprehension Strategies" chart.
- **USE THE FOUR STRATEGIES ABOVE TO COMPREHEND WHAT YOU READ.**

QUICK CONNECTIONS—CHAPTER TWO

News Source Connection

Using a news source (news magazine or newspaper), choose an article to read. Keep in mind that you are looking for the topic, the main idea and three important details. After reading the article, take three different colored highlighters and highlight the topic in one color, the main idea sentence in another color, and three important details in the third. If the main idea is not stated in a sentence, write your own main idea statement.

Textbook Connection

Use a textbook from one of your other classes, and if possible, do this activity as you are doing a reading assignment for the other class. Choose a section of the text and write the heading for that section on a sheet of paper. Scan the section for subheadings, and write those below the heading, leaving three lines between each subheading. As you read that section, fill in each of the three lines with an important detail from the section. If you do this for the entire assignment, you will have a complete set of study notes.

Novel Connection

After reading each chapter of a novel, stop to write down the topic of the chapter, the main idea, and at least three major details, or important things that happened. If you are unsure about the topic and/or main idea, write the details first, then see what they all relate to (topic), and what point is being made (main idea).

Computer Connection

Go to a news source website, such as *Time* magazine or the *New York Times* newspaper site. Choose an article that looks interesting and skim it to see what it's about. Write down what you *think* the topic and main idea of the article are. Read the article and then review what you initially wrote for the topic and main idea. Decide if your prediction was correct, and if not, rewrite what you now believe to be the topic and main idea. This is a good way to check your comprehension for any article you read.

Textbook Strategies

Chapter Preview

Textbook Strategies Overview

A. Identifying and Using Textbook Organizational Aids

B. Textbook Reading Methods
   1. SQ3R
   2. 3C
   3. Triple Highlighting

C. Skimming and Scanning

Course information bottom line . . .

The Textbook.

Objective

- Student will be able to successfully read a textbook by:
  1. Identifying and using textbook organizational aids
  2. Applying a textbook reading method
  3. Using the processes of skimming and scanning

Readiness Quiz

Choose **T** for true or **F** for false after reading each statement below.

1. _____ Most textbooks are set up in a similar way.

2. _____ In college, a student needs to read everything thoroughly.

3. _____ I've used highlighting to mark important information in a textbook.

4. _____ The index is the place to find the meaning of words used in a book.

5. _____ I normally read the preface in my textbooks.

6. _____ Skimming and scanning mean about the same thing.

7. _____ A reader who thoroughly reads the material once can remember most of the chapter.

8. _____ I have a method I use when I read textbooks.

9. _____ Scanning is used to get a quick overview of the reading material.

10. _____ When reading from a textbook, a reader should begin on the first page of the chapter and read until the chapter ends without skipping anything.

Textbook Strategies Overview

As a college student, it has been estimated that you will receive approximately 70 percent of the information you need to know from your textbooks. Therefore, it's extremely important that you know how to read your texts, comprehend them, gain the knowledge needed to pass your classes, and ultimately, to be successful in your career.

To achieve your textbook reading goals, there are three simple processes you can use. The first, identifying and using textbook organizational aids, is simply knowing what the aids are, being aware of them as you start each new textbook, and then using them to assure the most efficient reading of your textbooks. The five textbook aids you'll be learning about are the: Preface, Table of Contents, Glossary, Index, and Appendix.

The second process you'll learn is a method specifically designed for reading textbooks, which will enable you to get the most out of your book in the least amount of time. By now I'm sure you've discovered that trying to read a textbook the same way you read a novel or a newspaper just doesn't work! Because textbooks are fact dense, and because you're expected to remember much of the material, it takes an entirely different approach to read a text. Most readers have never been taught how to read textbooks. This results in a high rate of frustrated students and teachers. In this chapter you'll learn three methods for reading textbooks that are easy and really work! We've included three methods because students have different learning styles. Hopefully one of the methods, or a combination of them, will work for you. The three methods are: SQ3R, 3C, and triple highlighting.

The third textbook strategy that every college student can benefit from is a combination of two processes: skimming and scanning. You'll learn how to do both, and you'll also learn when to use these time-saving techniques.

Knowing and using the textbook strategies in this chapter can definitely make you a more successful college reader. Take the time to learn and practice these strategies until they become automatic. You'll be amazed at how much easier reading and comprehending your texts will become!

A. Identifying and Using Textbook Organizational Aids

Knowing where to locate and how to use five common parts of a textbook (called organizational aids) will make you a more efficient textbook reader. The five organizational aids in a text that are most useful to the student are the: Preface (also called To The Student), Table of Contents, Glossary, Index (Indexes), Appendix (Appendices). In addition to knowing these five parts, it's important to check each textbook for other textbook aids such as chapter previews and reviews, chapter objectives, summaries, headings and subheadings, visual and graphic aids, margin information, chapter questions and vocabulary aids.

QUICK TIP:

Always read the preface or To the Student section of your texts to quickly see what aids the author has included that will help you use that text more efficiently.

Your instructor may have you participate in an activity that will allow you to discover for yourself the five parts of a text mentioned above, and how each part can help you use your textbooks more efficiently. If your instructor chooses not to use the following activity with your class, complete it on your own with a text, or several texts, available to you.

QUICK TIP:

Start every school term by looking through each of your new textbooks to familiarize yourself with the organizational aids.

Textbook Organization and Aids

After being divided into groups and assigned one of the five text parts below, work as a group to fill in your section with a description of that part of a textbook. List the kinds of general information which would be found in that part of any textbook, not information specific to the text you're using. Complete your assigned part with your group and then fill in the others as each group presents.

Preface

_____

_____

_____

_____

_____

_____

Table of Contents

_____

_____

_____

_____

_____

_____

Glossary

_____

_____

_____

_____

_____

_____

Index(es)

_____

_____

_____

_____

_____

_____

Appendix (Appendices)

_____

_____

_____

_____

_____

Other Textbook Aids

_____

_____

_____

_____

_____

B. Textbook Reading Methods

As mentioned in the chapter introduction, it's a MUST for students to have a method, or strategy, for reading textbooks, since texts often differ greatly from any other kind of reading. Reading a textbook is like playing a football game. You would never be able to win the game if all you did was show up and play. There's much time spent before the game preparing, there's a plan for the actual playing time, and there's follow-up to make sure you learn from that game so you can do better in the next one. In order to "win" at reading textbooks, you need a plan that includes pregame preparation, playing strategies, and post-game follow-up.

We've included three different game strategies, or textbook reading methods. You'll notice that each has a pre-game (pre-reading) step, a playing (reading) plan, and a post-game (review) follow-up. Try each of them and see which one works best for you. You may want to combine parts of all three and come up with your own. What's important is that you have a method that works for YOU. Don't just show up to read and be a loser at the textbook reading game. Get your game plan, use it for every reading assignment, and be a winner at college textbook reading!

Here are brief explanations of the three text strategies. After you've read through them and have a basic understanding of how each one works, your instructor will provide you with several activities so you can try the strategies and determine which one, or which combination of the strategies, works best for you.

1. SQ3R

SQ3R (Survey, Question, Read, Recite, Review) has been one of the most popular text-reading strategies since World War II, when it was widely used by soldiers to learn the material in their training manuals. Many studies have been done on the effectiveness of SQ3R, all with results showing that students comprehend and retain more information when using SQ3R. SQ3R is an excellent textbook reading method for most students because it's easy to use, and it works! It works because it makes you *think* about what you're reading. Here's a brief explanation of the five steps in the SQ3R method.

SURVEY

Purpose: To become familiar with the overall content and organization of the material before you start reading. This enables you to comprehend faster and more thoroughly.

Method: Survey or preview the material by reading and **highlighting** the following:

- Title and subtitle
- Introduction (this can take several forms—chapter overview, chapter preview, chapter highlights, a list of main points in the chapter, or simply a paragraph)
- Headings and subheadings
- Bold or colored print, italics
- Margins
- Boxes
- Graphics (pictures, charts, graphs, diagrams, tables—and their captions)
- Vocabulary definitions
- Summary—end of chapter, end of sections—any summaries
- Questions—end of the chapter or sections—any questions

- Anything that catches your eye!!

- *Result:* A good survey gives you all of the most important information in a chapter and shows you how it's organized. This allows you to start comprehending as soon as you start to read.

QUICK TIP:

Surveying, plus reading once, has been proven more effective than reading a selection twice. Don't skip the survey!

QUESTION

Purpose: To give you something to think about before you start to read a section, and to give you something to look for as you read—the answer to your question. If you're looking for an answer, you stay more focused on the meaning of what you're reading.

Method: Make a question from each heading and subheading by using one of the W or H words (who, what, where, when, why, how). Write your W or H word lightly by the key word(s) in the heading. Most often your question will probably be "what is?" and then the heading. Your question should ask about the aspect of the heading that you're most curious about.

Result: You've created interest and now have a purpose for your reading—to find the answer to your question. Reading with interest and a purpose results in better attention to the content and improved comprehension.

QUICK TIP:

Use the 5 Ws and H to form questions from the headings.

READ

Purpose: To gain information and knowledge by finding the answer to your question.

Method: Read through the section under the heading looking for the answer to your question. Read only until you come to a new heading, then stop.

Result: You find the answer to your question, and your mind doesn't wander like it does when you read without a purpose. Also, you should understand and remember what you read because you're paying attention to it.

RECITE (HIGHLIGHT)

Purpose: To get a permanent record of the information you need to remember.

Method: Start by reciting (saying) and then highlighting the answer to the question you made from the heading. Recite and highlight names, dates, definitions, key parts of topic sentences, lists—everything you think might be on a test. After you've highlighted key information, you may also want to write yourself some notes in the margin to clarify certain passages, or to remind yourself of things you need to memorize, or things you need to ask your instructor. Remember that the key to good highlighting is never to try to highlight as you read material for the first time. Wait until you finish a section, then go back and highlight using the suggestions above.

Result: You now have a permanent record of the information you need to study for the test. From this point on you will only reread what you've highlighted, so make sure you think it's accurate and complete. If you are not able to, or don't want to highlight in the book, use one of the alternative methods of recording such as taking notes, outlining or mapping (Chapter 7), or try the 3C method, which is explained next.

QUICK TIP:

Only read from one heading to the next, and then STOP. Go back over what you just read and highlight the answer to your question, plus any other important information.

REVIEW

Purpose: To learn the material you need to know.

Method: Reread your highlighting at least three times. The first time to review is as soon as you've completed the reading. Check your highlighting at this time to make sure it's complete and accurate. The second time to reread your highlighting is every week, if possible, but at least once between finishing the assignment and starting to study for the test. The third time is before the test. Start rereading your highlighting several days before the test, and continue up to test time. Also memorize anything that you must know for sure from memory.

Result: You know everything you need to know from the text, and are ready to do well on your test.

> ## QUICK TIP:
>
> Reviewing is easy—just reread your highlighting and margin notes! The more often you read over them, the less studying you'll need to do right before a test.

2. 3C

3C was developed to give students a different way to break down and comprehend textbook material. This method uses 3×5 note cards, rather than highlighting, to record important information. It is based on the idea that the vocabulary and headings provide most of the key information in a textbook reading. There are times when you can't, or prefer not to, highlight in a book. Having your information on cards also makes studying more convenient because you can carry the cards with you and read over them whenever you have a few minutes of extra time. Hundreds of students have used 3C with a high degree of success.

CONNECT

Purpose: To connect with the content and organization of the chapter.

Method: Go through the chapter (takes approximately 10–15 minutes) and **look at** and **read** everything that catches your eye. This will include the title, headings, bold or color print, boxes or items in the margins, captions for all pictures, and charts and graphs. Skim (quickly read for main points) the summary and questions at the end of the chapter.

Result: This step will make it quicker and easier for you to comprehend because you'll get a good idea of what the chapter is about and you can start relating your background knowledge to the chapter content.

CARDS

Purpose: Most of the key information in a chapter is contained in the vocabulary and the headings. Using 3 × 5 note cards to define vocabulary words and write questions and answers from the headings gives you better comprehension and a record of the important information.

Method: Go through the chapter and do two things:

1. Make each bold heading into a question (similar to SQ3R). Then take a card and write that question on one side. Read to find the answer to your question, and when you find it, write it on the other side of the card.

2. Write each vocabulary word on a separate card and write the definition on the other side. In addition to the definition, writing a sentence containing the word will help you understand and remember the meaning of the word.

Result: You have a set of note cards containing the key information from the chapter.

QUICK TIP:

Draw a simple picture on the front (word and question) sides of your cards. The picture should be something that will trigger your memory of the definition or answer to your question. Your mind will remember the picture, and then the answer!

dissociative disorder	**Characterized by a person having a disruption, split or breakdown in his or her normal integrated self**

COMMIT TO MEMORY

Purpose: To learn the information for a test, for future courses, and/or your career.

Method: Carry your cards with you and read through them often. Take them with you to class and add important points your instructor makes.

Result: Frequent reading of the cards and self-testing will commit the information to your long-term memory and is easier and more effective than last-minute cramming.

QUICK TIP:

Get in the habit of carrying your cards with you wherever you go and remember to read through them any time you have a few extra minutes. Painless and efficient studying!

3. Triple Highlighting

Triple highlighting is a method that has been successfully used in college classes and the military. Air Force trainees using triple high-lighting were able to score at least 95 percent on a 100-question, closed-book test. Students in college classes found that the triple highlighted areas accurately predicted quiz questions. Triple high-lighting can be used with SQ3R and 3C if desired, or it can be used by itself. If you like triple highlighting better than the other two methods, be sure you still do some kind of survey, preview, or connection before you start reading. Also review and commit to memory the triple highlighted areas before a test. Here are the three steps in the triple highlighting method.

YELLOW HIGHLIGHT

Purpose: To record what you determine to be important information in the chapter.

Method: As you read, use a yellow highlighter to mark what you believe is important information.

Result: You have a record of the information you, the student, have determined to be important.

QUICK TIP:

Don't try to highlight as you're reading for the first time. Wait until the end of a section, then go back and highlight the important points. Everything seems important as you're reading—it's easier to see what's important when you have the complete picture.

BLUE HIGHLIGHT

Purpose: To record answers to questions posed by the author at the end of the chapter.

Method: If there are questions at the end of the chapter, find the answer to each question. With a pencil, write the number of the question in the margin next to the answer, then highlight the answer with blue.

Result: You have a record of the information the author has determined to be important.

PINK HIGHLIGHT

Purpose: To record important points emphasized by your instructor.

Method: Follow along in your text during class lecture and discussion. Notice when your instructor repeats points or writes them on the board. Highlight this information with pink.

Result: You have a record of the information your instructor has determined to be important.

TRIPLE HIGHLIGHT

Purpose: Shows you which information is most important and most likely to be on your tests.

Method: Reread everything that you've highlighted with all three colors. These areas contain the key information in the reading. The student (you!) thought it was important enough to highlight, the author thought it was important enough to write a question about, and the instructor thought it was important enough to emphasize in class. This means the likelihood of seeing that piece of information again on a test, or in some graded form, is very high.

Result: You have the most important information triple highlighted and ready to study for the test.

QUICK TIP:

Research has shown that triple highlighted information shows up on quizzes and tests a high percentage of the time.

Remember—reading a textbook is like playing a sport. If you just read, or play the game, without any preparation or follow-up work, you'll rarely win!

C. Skimming and Scanning

The last of our textbook reading strategies is actually two processes: skimming and scanning. There are different kinds of reading for different situations, even with textbook reading. You need to consider your *purpose* for reading to be able to decide which strategy to use. To get detailed information, using a text-reading strategy like SQ3R works best. But sometimes you don't need detailed information. You might be previewing or reviewing material. Or you might be looking for a specific piece of information. If your purpose is to get a quick overview of the material, or to preview or review, then skimming is the best method. If your purpose is to quickly find a certain fact or piece of information, scanning is the way to go. Neither of these methods requires the reading of every single word in the material, so they also serve as ways to speed up your reading—which is a good thing for college students.

Read the explanations of skimming and scanning that follow. Be sure you understand the difference between the two—both in the methods themselves, and also the purpose of each. Your instructor will provide you with several practice activities so you can become confident using skimming and scanning, and also confident that you know WHEN to use them.

QUICK TIP:

Stop and ask yourself **why** you're reading the material (your purpose) and then determine which reading strategy is needed.

Skimming

Skimming is used to quickly identify the main ideas of a text. When you read the newspaper, you probably don't read from front to back, word for word. Instead you read quickly over the headlines, and maybe the first few sentences of an article to get the main idea and/or to decide if you want to read the entire thing. If not, you continue to move your eyes quickly over the paper, reading the headlines and beginnings of articles. This is very similar to the techniques used in skimming. When you're done reading your newspaper, you have an overview of the news. When you skim an assignment, you have an overview of what it contains when you're done. This is often called a preview, or in SQ3R, the survey.

There are many strategies that can be used for skimming. Here are the most common ones—try them out and decide for yourself which ones work best for you.

How to Skim

- Read the title.
- Read the introduction or first paragraph.
- Read the chapter preview, overview, or highlights.
- Read the first sentence of each, or every other, paragraph.

- Read headings and subheadings.
- Notice pictures, charts, and graphs.
- Notice bold, italic or color words/phrases.
- Read the summary or last paragraph.

Now try skimming a reading assignment you have in a textbook, or an article in a news magazine to get an overview of the material.

QUICK TIP:

Skimming: **WHY?** To get a quick overview. **WHEN?** Before you start reading your assignment. **HOW?** See bulleted steps above.

Scanning

Scanning is completely different from skimming. You use scanning when you need to quickly locate a specific piece of information. You're using scanning when you look up a number in the telephone book, or a word in the dictionary. When you're skimming, you don't know what you're looking for—you're trying to determine what the reading is about. When you're scanning, you **do** know what you're looking for—a specific piece of information. In scanning you have a question in your mind, and you read a passage only to find the answer, ignoring unrelated information. Scanning involves moving your eyes quickly down the page, seeking specific words, phrases or numbers.

How to Scan

- State the specific information you're looking for.
- Anticipate how the answer will look—will it have capital letters at the beginning? Will it be a number? Is it one word or several words?
- Use headings and other aids to help you identify sections where your answer is most likely to appear.
- Move your eyes quickly down the page looking for the anticipated type of information.

Scan the following paragraph to find out how many moons Saturn has.

It's the start of a four-year tour, during which the ship will make at least 76 loops of the planet and engage a dozen cameras and instruments. NASA will be able to tweak the trajectory of the orbiter so it can slalom among nine of Saturn's 31 moons. The grandest of the satellites is Titan, which has long frustrated scientists because its dense atmosphere, laced with organic gases, obscures its surface.

(*Time*, June 28, 2004)

How many moons does Saturn have? Did you find the answer of 31? Were you looking for numerals rather than words? Good job! Now scan the paragraph again to find the answer to this question: How long is the ship's tour supposed to last?

What answer did you find for that question? The correct answer is four years, but the number was written out, and it was hyphenated to the word year, making it harder to find. Remember: If you can't find the answer to your question in the anticipated form, try to think of other ways it might appear. You might also look for another key word in the question, which in this case was the word "tour."

For more practice, go to the MRR website and click on skimming and scanning. This will provide you with practice skimming and scanning from a computer screen rather than from paper. You need to be able to do both.

QUICK TIP:

Scanning: **WHY?** To find specific information. **WHEN?** Only when you need the answer to a question. **HOW?** See the bulleted steps above.

Skimming and scanning are two easy ways you can improve your reading comprehension, efficiency, and speed. Remember to vary your reading speed and strategies according to your purpose.

QUICK TIP:

You don't need to, and shouldn't, read everything in college (or in life) word for word!

CHAPTER SUMMARY

- **TEXTBOOK STRATEGIES:** Approximately 70 percent of course information comes from the textbook. It's extremely important to know how to use textbooks and to have strategies for reading them.
- **TEXTBOOK ORGANIZATIONAL AIDS**
  - **Preface** — Author to reader, gives useful information about the book.
  - **Table of Contents** — Like an outline of the book, gives chapter titles, sections, page numbers.
  - **Glossary** — A mini-dictionary of words from the text with meanings as they are used in the text.
  - **Index (es)** — Alphabetical listing of topics in the book with page numbers showing where they can be found. Many textbooks have more than one index.
  - **Appendix (ices)** — Additional information in the back of the book. The text will refer you to the appendices. They're lettered A, B, C, etc.
- **TEXTBOOK READING METHODS**
  - **SQ3R** — A five-step method involving surveying, questioning, reading, reciting or highlighting and reviewing.
  - **3C** — A three-step method using index cards to record key information and vocabulary words and definitions.
  - **Triple Highlighting** — A three-step method using different color highlighters to mark important information as noted by the student, the author and the instructor.
- **SKIMMING AND SCANNING**
  - **Skimming** — Quickly reading over material to get the main idea of the entire reading.
  - **Scanning** — Quickly reading over material to find a specific piece of information.

QUICK CONNECTIONS—CHAPTER THREE

News Source Connection

Using a news source (news magazine or newspaper), choose an article that has several headings to read. Apply the SQ3R text-reading method to your news article. Surveying, making questions from the headings, highlighting the answers, and reviewing are also effective strategies to improve your reading of news articles with headings.

Textbook Connection

Use a textbook from one of your other classes, and if possible, do this activity as you are doing a reading assignment for the other class. Choose either SQ3R, 3C or triple highlighting, and read your assignment using the chosen textbook method. After you have finished, write down at least three things you liked about the method you used, and three things you didn't like. Do the same for each of the other two methods, and then you can determine which method (or perhaps a combination of the methods) works best for you.

Novel Connection

The first step of every textbook reading method involves a survey, or preview. Survey or preview the novel you will read before you start reading. In addition to the sections you preview for a textbook, see what other information is available to preview with your novel (i.e., book jacket). As with a textbook, a novel preview can improve comprehension. It can also help you get into the novel more *quick*ly.

Computer Connection

Conduct a search and find a site on the Internet where you can read about textbook reading methods and possibly find practices. Write a brief description of a textbook reading method that is new to you and seems to be one that would work well. Your instructor may have everyone in the class share the new method each student found. If you find a site with good practice exercises, use them to improve your textbook reading ability.

Critical Reading Strategies

Chapter Preview

Part A: Critical Reading Strategies Overview

A. Predicting, Making Inferences, and Drawing Conclusions
   1. Predicting
   2. Making Inferences and Drawing Conclusions

Part B: Critical Reading Strategies Overview

B. Analyzing and Synthesizing
   1. Identifying Writer's Purpose
   2. Fact and Opinion
   3. Judging Validity
   4. Identifying Author Attitude, Bias, Tone, and Assumptions

Reading can. . .

Take you places you might never go and introduce you to people you might never know.

STRATEGY AREA A: CRITICAL READING—PREDICTING, MAKING INFERENCES, AND DRAWING CONCLUSIONS

Objectives

- Student will be able to define critical reading.

- Student will be able to make predictions based on titles and passages read.

- Student will be able to make inferences based on information implied, but not stated, in a passage.

- Student will be able to draw conclusions from information presented in one or more passages.

Readiness Quiz A

Match the terms below with the best definitions on the right.

1. _____	critical	a. decide, determine
2. _____	imply	b. decide from suggestion
3. _____	infer	c. forecast or foretell
4. _____	conclude	d. evaluative
5. _____	explicit	e. suggest
6. _____	predict	f. clearly stated

Questions for Discussion

What is critical reading?

How do you read critically?

PART A: CRITICAL READING STRATEGIES OVERVIEW

A. Predicting, Making Inferences, and Drawing Conclusions

While the word *critical* has various dictionary definitions, when used in the context of critical reading, the term generally involves higher order thinking strategies such as analyzing, comparing, and judging. It is *evaluative* and reflective in nature. As used in the context of this chapter, it refers to any higher order thinking and reading strategies.

Critical thinking and reading are challenging and complex processes. There are entire courses devoted to these topics. This chapter is not meant to thoroughly cover this area. It is merely a starting point. Critical reading requires continual exposure to a variety of written materials, and consistent practice. The practices in this text should be followed up with ongoing practice. Participating in classroom discussions can also be helpful to you as you are exposed to the various perspectives and backgrounds of experience shared among your classmates. Broadening your own background of experience and expanding your perspectives will allow you to read and think more critically.

The first part of this chapter focuses on the critical reading strategies of predicting, making inferences, and drawing conclusions, which require higher level thinking. The latter two strategies often overlap. It's generally necessary to draw a conclusion in order to make an inference. However, not all conclusions require you to make an inference. We'll begin with strategies for predicting.

1. Predicting

Effective readers are active readers. They begin making predictions about what will come next—right from the beginning of a reading, starting with the title if there is one. Being aware of a writer's pattern of organization (see Chapter Six) may help you to anticipate the direction a writing will take. Test questions sometimes ask the reader to extend (extrapolate or project on the basis of known information) into the future or into a new situation. To make such "predictions," you must first have a clear understanding of the passage. Next, build upon this information by analyzing the logic used by the writer and/or the sequence of events described. Then, make choices that are consistent with the passage, but that do not *over*extend or stretch the ideas expressed there.

QUICK TIP:

Notice the way people are described. Use information about their personalities, thoughts, or feelings to determine how they might act or react.

QUICK TIP:

After reading and analyzing a passage, ask yourself what might happen as a result of the stated actions or events.

Using the previewing strategy while reading can serve as a major step toward making more accurate predictions. Another great tool involves treating the reading as if it were a two-way conversation. In other words, after each statement a writer makes, the reader can practice an internal dialogue, responding to each point. This strategy simulates what happens in a face-to-face conversation. When you are listening to someone, you generally respond in some way to demonstrate that you have listened and understood. You may ask questions along the way to encourage the speaker to clarify or amplify (expand) what has been said. Active reading, much like active listening, enables you to get much more out of the communication and also to retain it more effectively.

Consider this title: *The Story of an Hour*

When you read this title, what expectations do you have for the information that will follow? You may or may not be accurate, depending upon many factors, but you will be more prepared for what follows if you at least attempt to anticipate or predict what lies ahead. You would obviously expect some type of story that takes place within an hour. Your internal dialogue might go something like this: "The Story of an Hour . . . hmm, good, that might mean it's not going to be very long. I wonder how someone can make much of a story out of something that only takes an hour. Well, I guess I'll find out."

Don't underestimate the importance of starting to predict by questioning or reflecting upon the title. Sometimes students are in such a hurry that they neglect to pay much attention to the title, or to do a quick preview of the reading. Taking the time to predict can save time later because you get more out of what you read. Continue the active internal dialogue throughout a reading, and you will be well on your way toward making better predictions.

Now complete a brief practice as you read this short excerpt from Yann Martel's 2001 novel, *Life of Pi*. Pi, the main character in the book, is giving some advice to those who might happen to fall into a lion's pit at a zoo. Try writing short responses where indicated (by the blank lines) within the passage. Then check suggested answers below. To get you started, one possible response for question 1 below might be: "If I fall into a lion's pit? How would that happen? Maybe during a visit to the zoo." Now see if you can come up with your own thoughts and write them on the lines below.

1. So you see, if you fall into a lion's pit,

_____

2. the reason the lion will tear you to pieces

_____

3. is not because it's hungry—

_____

4. be assured, zoo animals are amply fed—

_____

5. or because it's bloodthirsty,

_____

6. but because you've invaded its territory.

_____

Answers will vary, but the following are some possibilities:

1. Well, I don't intend to ever do that, but if I did, what should I know?
2. Tear me to pieces? Does the lion need a reason? Isn't that just what lions do?

3. Oh, I didn't really think the lion would need to be hungry to tear me to pieces, but what would his reason be, according to you?

4. Yes, I suppose they are, so go on . . .

5. It's not? I guess I thought lions were bloodthirsty. Now you've really got me curious.

6. Oh, yes, I would have invaded its territory. Lions are just protecting their territory then . . . like some people do. Interesting!

FINAL PRACTICE ON PREDICTING

Now you're ready for the last practice exercise for this section. Try predicting, using an excerpt from the textbook *Keys to Business Success*, by Martha Doran (2000). Consider this heading from the chapter Business Communication:

HOW DO NONVERBAL CLUES GIVE MEANING IN COMMUNICATION?

1. Can you predict what minor headings might be included under a heading on nonverbal clues?

   _____

   _____

   A paragraph under the heading *GESTURES* begins with this sentence: "We usually consider gestures as obvious, yet they are culturally bound."

2. What would you predict to follow this introductory sentence? Write your thoughts below. Then read the entire paragraph which follows.

   _____

   _____

   _____

We usually consider gestures as obvious, yet they are culturally bound. An American's friendly wave with the left hand to say "hi" may be an insult in some cultures where the left hand is considered unclean (the hygiene or toilet hand). The American "thumbs up" gesture to indicate OK is an obscene gesture in other cultures. While Americans may nod their heads up and down to indicate agreement, people in another culture nod the head to indicate no; while Americans shake their heads left to right to indicate no, in another culture the head turns to the left to indicate yes. Differing interpretations of gestures lead to the cultural aversion to foreigners who appear insulting and uncouth to the host culture. Since Americans frequently travel abroad, they may unwittingly communicate a poor image of themselves with wrong gestures. Most likely, they will not realize the wrong message, since that message is what the host culture perceives, not the in-tended message of the gesture.

How did you do? Discuss possible answers with your class.

2. Making Inferences and Drawing Conclusions

An **inference** is an idea that is clearly *suggested* or *implied* by a writer, al-though not *explicitly* stated. When making inferences, keep in mind the main idea and details of a passage. You should be able to defend your in-ference by first pointing to clearly stated information in a passage, and then reading "between the lines."

Making inferences is a natural part of the thinking process. For in-stance, if you pass a friend or acquaintance in a hallway and greet that person, but fail to get a response to your greeting, you probably infer something like "she must not have seen me" or "he must be preoccupied right now" or "gee, she's really stuck up!" The tricky thing about infer-ences is that, because they are implied, it's possible to be wrong. Perhaps the acquaintance didn't recognize you. Or possibly the friend had just received traumatic news and was too emotional to respond. The more evidence or clues you have to make an accurate inference, the better.

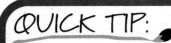

QUICK TIP:

Use the "if–then" test to verify your inference. Does it make sense that if X (information stated in the passage) is true, then Y (your inference) is probably true?

When attempting to **draw conclusions** (including making inferences), be sure you first understand the main idea and details of a passage. Also use context clues, other vocabulary strategies, and a dictionary to clar-ify any difficult terminology. Keep in mind the sequence of events and/or logical reasoning. Determine what might result from the actions or events the writer has described. Allow your own background of experi-ence or prior knowledge to help you draw a conclusion without reading too much into a passage or overextending its content.

QUICK TIP:

Determine a consequence that is consistent with the content of the passage by mentally adding your response to the end of the reading and asking if it fits logically.

Consider this passage from the beginning of Dave Pelzer's (1995) autobiographical novel:

> SMACK! *Mother hits me in the face and I topple to the floor. I know better than to stand there and take the hit. I learned the hard way that she takes that as an act of defiance, which means more hits, or worst of all, no food. I regain my posture and dodge her looks, as she screams into my ears.*
>
> *A Child Called "It"*

What inferences can you make regarding the situation described above? The passage doesn't need to tell us directly that this is an ongoing, abusive relationship between a mother and her son. We quickly infer these things. We might also infer that the child is perceptive enough to have learned how best to deal with the abuse. We get a glimpse of the importance of food to this child since "no food" is worse than "more hits." These inferences all fit the context of the passage. We might begin predicting what will follow, but any serious predictions at this point in the book would overextend the information given. As the story unfolds, we can begin to more accurately draw conclusions and make predictions because we have a stronger base of context from which to do this.

Now read the following excerpt:

> *Stacey's story is enough to make any parent sick with worry. Sadly, her experience is growing more common. Over the last year, local and federal law-enforcement officials say they have noted a marked increase in teen prostitution in cities across the country. Solid numbers are difficult to come by—a government-sponsored study puts the figure in the hundreds of thousands—but law-enforcement agencies and advocacy groups that work with teen prostitutes say they are increasingly alarmed by the trend lines: the kids are getting younger; according to the FBI, the average age of a new recruit is just 13; some are as young as 9. The girls—many fewer are boys, most experts believe—are subjected to more*

violence from pimps. And, while the vast majority of teen prostitutes today are runaways, illegal immigrants and children of poor urban areas, experts say a growing number now come from middle-class homes.

(*Newsweek*, "This Could Be Your Kid," August 2003)

Since this passage is taken out of context, the reader might infer that "Stacey's story" either came before . . . or would follow. The information seems to indicate that Stacey may be one of those teens involved in teen prostitution. However, without more information, it's possible, for example, that Stacey was merely approached by a pimp. We can also infer that parents who need to be the most concerned are those whose children have run away, are illegal immigrants, live in poor urban areas, or come from middle class homes. While it is logical for the reader to draw this conclusion, it would not be logical to draw the conclusion that *only* these parents need be concerned. Such a conclusion would overextend the content of the passage.

INFERENCES PRACTICE

Try a paragraph from a developmental psychology textbook. Read the passage, then answer the questions that follow:

Newborns appear to respond differentially to all four of the basic flavors (Crook, 1987). Some of the clearest demonstrations of this come from an elegantly simple set of early studies by Jacob Steiner (Ganchrow et al., 1983; Steiner, 1979). Newborn infants who had never been fed were photographed before and after flavored water was put into their mouths. By varying the flavor, Steiner could determine whether the babies reacted differently to different tastes. . . babies responded quite differently to sweet, sour, and bitter flavors.

(Bee, 2000)

Place a checkmark in front of the inferences it is possible to make from this passage:

1. _____ Responses to taste are merely learned responses.
2. _____ Newborn babies probably display a negative reaction to a bitter taste.
3. _____ It's likely that the passage will go on to address newborns' reactions to smell.
4. _____ Since this research began in 1979, it is probably outdated.
5. _____ The flavored water used posed danger to the newborns.

DRAWING CONCLUSIONS PRACTICE
For the final exercise in this section, compare two passages from separate websites which comment on the celebration of Columbus Day. Read
both passages, then answer the questions that follow.

Passage 1

*Historically, Columbus was not the first to discover America, nor was he the first
European to land at America. He was the first to exploit, kill, and enslave the
Arawak Indians of Haiti. The myth of Christopher Columbus and the discovery
of America is due to Washington Irving. His "biography" of Columbus was pop-
ularized in a dramatic and embellished account. In recent years, the holiday has been
rejected by many people who view it as a celebration of conquest and genocide. In
its place, Indigenous Peoples Day is celebrated.*

(www.bright.net/~jimsjems/columbus.html)

Passage 2

*The politically correct view is that Columbus did not discover America, because peo-
ple had lived here for thousands of years. Worse yet, it's claimed, the main legacy
of Columbus is death and destruction. Columbus is routinely vilified as a symbol
of slavery and genocide, and the celebration of his arrival likened to a celebration
of Hitler and the Holocaust. The attacks on Columbus are ominous, because the
actual target is Western civilization.*

*Did Columbus "discover" America? Yes—in every important respect. This does
not mean that no human eye had been cast on America before Columbus arrived.
It does mean that Columbus brought America to the attention of the civilized world,
i.e., to the growing, scientific civilizations of Western Europe. The result, ultimately,
was the United States of America. It was Columbus' discovery for Western Europe
that led to the influx of ideas and people on which this nation was founded—and on
which it still rests. The opening of America brought the ideas and achievements of Aris-
totle, Galileo, Newton, and the thousands of thinkers, writers, and inventors who
followed.*

(www.aynrand.org/objectivism/columbus.html)

Now answer these questions:

1. Would you conclude that these two writers agree or disagree?

   _____

2. Which passage would most likely support the celebration of Columbus Day?

   _____

3. List words that enable the reader to "hear" the emotion of the writer in passage 1. In other words, which words may have been used by the writer to trigger an emotional response from the reader? (Example: 'exploit' has a negative connotation. Refer to discussion on connotative language in Chapter One, Vocabulary Strategies.)

---

4. List words that enable the reader to "hear" the emotion of the writer in passage 2.

STRATEGY AREA B: CRITICAL READING—ANALYZING AND SYNTHESIZING

Objectives

- Student will be able to identify writer's purpose.

- Student will be able to distinguish between a fact and an opinion.

- Student will be able to judge the validity of supporting evidence.

- Student will be able to identify author attitudes, bias, tone, and assumptions.

Readiness Quiz B1

Write an **F** before the statements which are facts and an **O** before the statements which are opinions.

1. _____ Jennifer Lopez is beautiful.

2. _____ George Washington was the second President of the United States.

3. _____ College tuition rates in Nebraska are on the rise.

4. _____ Nebraska state taxes are too high.

5. _____ A U.S. President was impeached.

6. _____ Investing in the stock market is risky.

Readiness Quiz B2

Part a: Match the terms below with the correct definitions on the right.

1. _____ valid

2. _____ evidence

3. _____ attitude

4. _____ assumption

5. _____ predict

6. _____ bias

a. the act of taking for granted without proof

b. a position or manner indicative of feeling, opinion, or intention toward a person or thing

c. foretell

d. the means of proving or disproving an assertion

e. subjective point of view

f. well supported by fact

Part b: Choose **T** for true or **F** for false after reading each statement below.

1. _____ A writer's attitude must be either positive or negative.

2. _____ Readers should always refrain from making predictions based upon a reading unless the prediction is stated within the passage.

3. _____ It's possible to recognize unstated ideas a writer accepts as true or takes for granted.

4. _____ A writer may present evidence that is true, but does not actually support his/her argument.

5. _____ The tone of a reading is the underlying feeling the writer creates.

6. _____ It is impossible to determine a writer's purpose unless it's directly stated.

PART B: CRITICAL READING STRATEGIES OVERVIEW

B. Analyzing and Synthesizing

In addition to predicting, making inferences, and drawing conclusions, readers are often required to analyze (break down or dissect) and synthesize (arrange or blend) information. It may be necessary to determine a writer's purpose, separate facts from opinions, judge the validity of an argument, and/or identify an author's attitudes, bias, tone, and assumptions, based on information presented.

1. Identifying the Writer's Purpose

A key element of better comprehension is for the reader to discern the writer's purpose and intended audience. Writers usually have a specific purpose and audience in mind when writing. The purpose will determine how a reading is organized and will also influence the writer's word choices.

Sometimes clues to the writer's purpose will be evident in the title of a reading. Some writers will directly state the purpose. Often, however, the purpose is not stated, but merely implied. The reader's careful attention to word choices in the titles, headings, and reading will usually pay off in improved understanding of the writer's purpose. And understanding the purpose will greatly enhance the reader's comprehension of the main idea and details of the reading.

Main purposes of a reading may include the following:

- To inform
- To describe
- To persuade
- To entertain
- To narrate (tell a story)

It's important to realize, however, that although a reading usually has one main purpose, the writer may include a variety or mix of minor purposes as well. For a more detailed analysis of some of these (and other) purposes, see Chapter 6, Patterns of Organization Strategies.

WRITER'S PURPOSE PRACTICE

Read the short passages below, and try to determine which of the following is the writer's main purpose: to inform, describe, persuade, entertain, or narrate.

> *The young woman was tall, with a figure of perfect elegance on a large scale. She had dark and abundant hair, so glossy that it threw off the sunshine with a gleam, and a face which, besides being beautiful from regularity of feature and richness of complexion, had the impressiveness belonging to a marked brow and deep black eyes. She was ladylike, too, after the manner of the feminine gentility of those days . . .*

> (Hawthorne, 1959)

Main purpose: _____

> *Think you might have HIV? Several sites around Omaha will offer free, confidential testing for a virus that is particularly affecting blacks and Latinos and is making a comeback in white gay men. "It's on the rise in all communities," said Rosey Higgs, HIV testing and counseling coordinator at the Nebraska AIDS Project. Federal health experts estimate that 180,000 to 280,000 HIV-positive people in the United States do not know their status . . . Free tests are available Friday, Saturday, and Monday.*

> (Adapted from the *Omaha World Herald*, 2005)

Main purpose: _____

2. Fact and Opinion

Critical readers need to be able to differentiate between facts and opinions. A fact is an idea that can be proved or disproved. An idea can be a fact even if it is untrue, as long as it can be either proved or disproved (see Readiness Quiz B1, question 2). Opinions usually include words which **interpret** (*explain or show the meaning of*) or **evaluate** (*judge the value of*) something. Sentence number one below is a clear statement of fact; the second sentence reflects an evaluation.

1. The woman who applied for the job had blue eyes and shoulder-length brown hair.
2. A beautiful woman applied for the job.

It's someone's opinion that the woman is beautiful. While there are numerous examples of interpretive words, here are a few more: loving, dangerous, bad, attractive, gentle, improper, brilliant, finest.

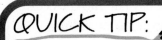

QUICK TIP:

Look for words that **interpret** or **evaluate.** These often indicate an opinion.

Some words clearly indicate that an opinion follows. Examples: *I feel, I think, I believe, in my opinion.* Other words like *possibly, probably, usually, sometimes, often* or *perhaps* may be used to limit a statement and to allow for the possibility of other viewpoints. Opinions may be valid when properly supported, and *facts* may actually be false.

QUICK TIP:

Look for words that act as clues to statements of opinion.

Some people think that in order for something to be a fact, it must be proven scientifically. The scientific method, however, can only be used to prove repeatable observations. Another method for proving a fact is called legal-historical proof. This kind of proof depends upon exhibits, oral testimony, and written testimony. An example of this type of fact would be that George Washington was the first President of the United States. Such a statement cannot be proved scientifically, yet is a fact based on legal-historical proof.

One other caution when distinguishing between facts and opinions relates to making predictions. Since the future can't be proved by any method, predictions are regarded as opinions.

FACT AND OPINION PRACTICE

Consider the following statements in light of the discussion above. Write **F** for *facts* and **O** for *opinions:*

1. _____ American children watch too much television.

2. _____ Abraham Lincoln was the sixteenth President of the United States.

3. _____ Women are better communicators than men.

4. _____ The state of California will one day fall into the ocean.

5. _____ Mount Rainier in Washington State is 14,410 feet high.

Even experts' opinions may vary. For instance, some doctors promote a high protein, low carbohydrate diet, while other doctors remain skeptical. Some opinions are so widely accepted that they may seem like facts. However, when interpretation or evaluation is involved, statements are generally considered opinions.

The following passage is from an editorial. Identify as many of the interpretive or evaluative words (or phrases) as you can find, and mark or underline them in the passage. Then check the key below it.

> *The rules for who must be paid overtime in America are more complicated than they need to be, and many of the job categories are hopelessly outmoded, having been crafted in some cases as long as 65 years ago. Few could doubt that such a situation needed clarifying.*
>
> *But in regard to the foreign workers, a terrible message is being sent, asking Congress to endorse law-breaking by millions of people. They sneak across the borders, usually entering a shadowy world of shabby housing, tax evasion and fear of almost all law enforcement. Most deserve better than that.*
>
> Omaha World Herald ("Straight Talk on Jobs," January 8, 2004)

KEY: The following words should be marked or underlined: complicated, outmoded, needed clarifying, terrible, sneak, shadowy, shabby, fear, deserve better.

3. Judging Validity

A crucial component of judging the **validity** of evidence (that is, evidence well supported by facts) is to examine the *source* of the evidence. Determine whether or not the source represents expertise, research, and/or appropriate data. Next, look at the evidence itself. Evidence that supports a conclusion strengthens an argument, while evidence that contradicts or casts doubt on a conclusion weakens an argument. Review a writer's claim as well as the evidence used to support it.

QUICK TIP:

Test possible facts to determine if examples provided directly affect the logical chain of reasoning and are, therefore, valid evidence or sound proof.

QUICK TIP:

Ask yourself if a new piece of evidence strengthens the writer's claim, weakens the writer's claim, or is irrelevant to the validity (soundness) of the claim.

It's important to determine if a writer has used sound reasoning to develop a logical argument. Do the thoughts flow logically, or are there missing connections between ideas presented? Has the writer been complete in supporting a conclusion? Do any of the writer's claims contradict each other?

How about the author's use of language? Are words chosen to appeal to the reader's emotions rather than one's sense of logic? Is the language ambiguous (vague or unclear)?

Another important strategy for judging the validity of an argument is to look for common fallacies (false or erroneous ideas) in the reasoning. **While there are at least hundreds of fallacies in logic and they may often overlap, several of the most common are as follows:**

Emotional appeal: Words, phrases, slogans, or images are used to arouse a favorable response from the reader. Such tactics can be used in advertisements and political campaigns, or in any kind of persuasive writing. Readers need to look beyond the emotional appeal to consider the true validity of the argument.

Examples
A politician uses terms like *freedom* and *the American way* in a persuasive essay. Controversial issues like gay rights and abortion are discussed using positive or negative terms (homophobic, pro-life, anti-choice) to sway the reader, apart from the facts. (See discussion on connotative language in Chapter One, Vocabulary.)

Attack the person, or name-calling: A person's conclusion is ignored or attacked on the basis of something the person has (or has not) done or said, rather than on the basis of that person's argument. Such fallacies are rampant during political campaigns, but can occur frequently whenever people differ in their perspectives. Attacks on a person and name-calling are used to divert the reader's attention from the real issue.

Examples
Senator X is a left-wing liberal, so why should we listen to anything he has to say?

Mrs. Y claims that teachers aren't doing their jobs, but since she's never been a teacher, how would she know?

Hasty generalization: A conclusion is drawn without sufficient evidence or from too small a sample.

Examples
Several police officers in Los Angeles beat up a black man during an arrest. Therefore, the L.A. Police Department is racist.

A pro-life activist shoots and kills an abortionist. Therefore, pro-lifers are dangerous right-wing extremists.

All or nothing: Opinions that state or imply the word *all* are generally stereotypes (and similar to hasty generalizations). They often ignore individual differences or relevant data.

Examples
Lawyers are greedy.

All men are insensitive.

Women are more emotional than men.

Children today are spoiled and lazy.

False cause: Many issues are complex. In an attempt to arrive at a conclusion, events are often erroneously linked as having a cause–effect relationship. The fact that one event follows another does not necessitate such a relationship. An outcome may also be the result of multiple causes, not just one.

Examples
No wonder crime is on an upswing; look at all the violence on TV. While violence on TV *may* contribute to the crime rate, the issue is more complicated. Also, it's important to determine if the initial claim—crime is on an upswing—is true before looking at the validity of the causes.

When some children get taller, they get worse grades in school. The lower grades could actually be caused by factors such as increased activities, hormonal issues, higher expectations, or peer pressure.

Testimonial: A famous person endorses a product (or service). People can be swayed by the fame of the person, rather than by the merit of the product.

Examples
Michael Jordan advertises a particular brand of athletic shoes.

Candice Bergen promotes a cellular phone.

Now read the following passage from a website article on school uniforms:

> *If people were taught to appreciate and enjoy difference instead of avoid it and compete against it, maybe there would be fewer conflicts in this world. Anyone who can only "work together to achieve a common goal" with people who look the same is seriously crippled. Students who "behave better" in uniforms are being taught that uniformity is essential to productivity. New ideas are more often than not bad ideas. But if we didn't think of new ideas, we would never have good ideas. We must encourage diversity and work with the bad ideas to achieve the good ones, which are usually "out there." But in a room full of clones, who wants to risk putting forward an "out there" idea?*

> *People don't look the same, and we have to learn to accept that. If we want to train our kids to "join the workforce" in the offices downtown, then sure, they're never too young to wear the uniform. (Why not start preschoolers on time clock cards?) But if we want to show kids that there are more important*

things than how they dress, we should show them that how they dress doesn't matter.

People raised uniformly will think, act, work, and live uniformly. Arguments for the "benefits" of conformity are aimed at people who will not think critically about those arguments—people who were probably raised in uniforms anyway.

(www.babelloyd.com/likeitis0035.html)

Since this excerpt is taken out of context, the purpose of this next activity is not to criticize the writer, but to practice looking for fallacies (false or erroneous ideas) in the reasoning. Which fallacies can you identify for each of the statements below? (You may find more than one for each.)

Fallacy Practice

1. Anyone who can only "work together to achieve a common goal" with people who look the same is seriously crippled.

_____

2. New ideas are more often than not bad ideas.

_____

3. People raised uniformly will think, act, work, and live uniformly.

_____

4. Identifying Author Attitude, Bias, Tone, and Assumptions

Careful readers will attempt to discern a writer's attitude toward a subject, as well as to *uncover* assumptions a writer has made. The attitude a writer takes toward a subject is often expressed through the use of positive or negative words. (See discussion on connotative language in Chapter One, Vocabulary.) A reader's awareness and analysis of word choices will be a major step toward exposing any bias the writer has expressed toward a topic.

When the writer is objective, word choices will often be neutral and/or both sides of an issue will be covered. When the writer expresses his or her own ideas or feelings about a topic, or covers only one side of an issue, the point of view is biased. This type of writing is considered subjective, rather than objective. Besides enabling the reader to pick up on any bias the writer has expressed, word choices used by the writer also help the reader to interpret the tone of the message. The tone may vary throughout a message, and involve an underlying feeling such as humor, anger, or fear.

QUICK TIP:

Look for clue words in a passage that signal a writer's attitude toward a subject.

Examples of positive words: enthusiastic, patriotic, sympathetic, admirable, brave, caring, excellent

Examples of negative words: nasty, sarcastic, unfortunate, inadequate, inept, disapproving, substandard

Writers might express, for example, anger, humor, respect, impatience, sympathy, or disapproval. Or they might exhibit a neutral attitude. Pay close attention to word choices.

Opinions often flow from a writer's assumptions. Assumptions are ideas or perspectives that underlie a writer's claim. They sometimes result in stereotypes. Since assumptions are usually unstated and implied, they can be challenging to uncover. Consider the following example:

Orca whales mate for life and travel in family groups.

Science has demonstrated that Orca whales are intelligent.

Therefore, Orca whales should be saved from extinction.

The underlying assumption is that *an animal that displays such human qualities warrants special protection.* Unless the reader agrees with the underlying assumption, the evidence presented may not be valid for that reader.

QUICK TIP:

Sometimes, you might identify a *missing* piece in the writer's logic that helps uncover an assumption.

Picking up on an author's attitudes and assumptions usually requires the reader to make inferences and draw conclusions (see the beginning of the chapter). Consider the following statement from a passage comparing human and animal cultures:

> Our culture lets us make up for having lost our strength, claws, long teeth, and other defenses.

What assumption has the writer made?

_____

The underlying assumption is that *humans evolved from animals*. If the reader agrees with this assumption, it may be more difficult to uncover the assumption. However, for a reader who does not accept the theory of evolution, such a statement may stand out and cause the reader to question the validity of the argument.

ATTITUDE, BIAS, TONE, AND ASSUMPTION PRACTICE

The following is a paragraph from the 1960 novel, *Night*, by Elite Wiesel. Wiesel is struggling with his faith in God as a result of his experience in concentration camps during the Holocaust. These are his thoughts.

> *"Blessed be the Name of the Eternal!"*
>
> *Why, but why should I bless Him? In every fiber I rebelled. Because He had had thousands of children burned in His pits? Because He kept six crematories working night and day, on Sundays and feast days? Because in His great might He had created Auschwitz, Birkenau, Buna, and so many factories of death? How could I say to Him: "Blessed art Thou, Eternal, Master of the Universe, Who chose us from among the races to be tortured day and night, to see our fathers, our mothers, our brothers, end in the crematory? Praised be Thy Holy Name, Thou Who hast chosen us to be butchered on Thine altar?"*

1. What assumptions is Wiesel making in this passage?

   _____

2. How would you describe Wiesel's attitude toward God in the passage above? What words or phrases used in the paragraph support your response?

Attitude: _____

Supportive words or phrases: _____

3. What other words might you use to describe the overall tone of this passage?

_____

4. Is Wiesel expressing a biased or a neutral point of view?

_____

CHAPTER SUMMARY

- **CRITICAL THINKING:** Generally involves higher order thinking skills such as analyzing, comparing, and judging. It is *evaluative* and reflective in nature. As used in the context of this chapter, it refers to any higher order thinking and reading skills.

- **PREDICTING:** Previewing a reading, beginning with the title, is a major step toward making more accurate predictions. Notice the way people are described, and after reading and analyzing a passage, ask yourself what might happen as a result of the stated actions or events.

- **MAKING INFERENCES:** An idea that is clearly *suggested* or *implied* by a writer, although not *explicitly* stated. When making inferences, keep in mind the main idea and details of a passage. Use the if–then test to verify inferences.

- **DRAWING CONCLUSIONS:** It's generally necessary to draw a conclusion in order to make an inference. However, not all conclusions require you to make an inference. Determine a consequence that is consistent with the content of the passage by mentally adding your response to the end of the reading and asking if it fits logically.

- **ANALYZING AND SYNTHESIZING:** Readers are often required to analyze (break down or dissect) and synthesize (arrange or blend) information.

- **WRITER'S PURPOSE:** Writers usually have a specific purpose and audience in mind, which often determines the organizational pattern and words choices used. Main purposes of a reading may be to **inform,** to **describe,** to **persuade,** to **entertain,** or to **narrate.**

- **FACT AND OPINION:** A fact is an idea that can be proved or disproved. An idea can be a fact even if it is untrue, as long as it can be either proved or disproved. Opinions usually include words which <u>interpret</u> (*explain or show the meaning of*) or <u>evaluate</u> (*judge the value of*) something.

- **JUDGING VALIDITY:** First determine if the **source** represents expertise, research, and/or appropriate data. Then decide if the

evidence strengthens the writer's claim, weakens the writer's claim, or is irrelevant to the validity of the claim. Make sure that arguments used flow logically and avoid contradictions. Look for common **fallacies** such as emotional appeals and all-or-nothing thinking.

- **IDENTIFYING AUTHOR ATTITUDE, BIAS, TONE, AND ASSUMPTIONS:** Look for **clue words** in a passage that signal a writer's attitude toward a subject. Begin with titles and headings. Be on the lookout for assumptions (ideas or perspectives that underlie a writer's claim). These are often challenging to uncover because they tend to be unstated or implied.

QUICK CONNECTIONS—CHAPTER FOUR

News Source Connection

Using a news source (news magazine or newspaper), choose a persuasive article or an editorial to read. Find and mark (or list) two to three conclusions or claims the writer has made. Then try to identify supporting evidence the writer has used, and evaluate the validity of the claims. Also attempt to identify any assumptions the writer has made.

Textbook Connection

Use a textbook from one of your other classes, and if possible, do this activity as you are completing a reading assignment for the other class. Choose a section of the text you haven't yet read, and write the heading for that section on a sheet of paper. Based solely on that heading, identify two or more questions you expect the following section of text to answer. Then continue reading to find out if your *predictions* were accurate.

Novel Connection

After reading at least one chapter of a novel, identify two main characters. Draw conclusions about these characters, and list four or five character traits for each. (Examples might include words like *humorous, outgoing, stubborn, angry,* or *loving.*) For each trait listed, identify a line or passage in the chapter that supports your conclusions.

Computer Connection

Go to a news source website, such as *Newsweek* or the *New York Times* site. Choose an article that looks interesting, and skim it to make sure it includes both facts and opinions. List three statements of fact and three statements of opinion that you found (or print the article and highlight or mark them).

Figurative Language Strategies

Chapter Preview
Figurative Language Strategies Overview

A. Metaphor and Simile

B. Personification

C. Hyperbole

True Story . . .
A mother asked her young son to "keep an eye on" his baby brother. The son looked confused and asked, "but mommy, how do I take it out?"

Objective

- Student will be able to recognize these four common types of figurative language, and interpret them when used in context:

  1. Metaphor

  2. Simile

  3. Personification

  4. Hyperbole

Readiness Quiz A

Match the terms below with the correct definitions on the right.

1. _____ simile	a. human qualities attributed to an object, animal, or idea
2. _____ metaphor	b. a deliberate overstatement or exaggeration
3. _____ personification	c. using *like* or *as* to make a comparison between two things
4. _____ hyperbole	d. symbolical, not literal
5. _____ figurative	e. making a comparison between two things without using *like* or *as*

Readiness Quiz B

Now match the terms below with the correct examples on the right.

1. _____ simile	a. The tulips danced in the breeze.
2. _____ metaphor	b. She's as lovely as a bright spring day.
3. _____ personification	c. He's at least a thousand years old.
4. _____ hyperbole	d. We peered out upon a fluffy, white blanket of snow.

Figurative Language Strategies Overview

This chapter focuses on four common types of figurative language: simile, metaphor, personification, and hyperbole. Figurative language is frequently used in poetry and other types of literature, but may show up in any kind of writing. It can greatly enhance the imaginative element of the reading process and, therefore, create some challenges in interpretation. At the same time, figurative language can assist the reader in understanding and making connections between the writer's thoughts and the reader's world of experience. Figurative language often invokes imagination rather than literal interpretation. Recognizing and understanding common forms of figurative language improves the reader's ability to make appropriate interpretations and applications of the language. You may rarely need to identify the actual figurative language terms, so focus on recognizing these common figures of speech and allowing them to help you draw connections the writer is implying.

QUICK TIP:

When you recognize a writer's use of figurative language, attempt to create pictures in your mind of images the writer is "painting" for the reader.

A. Metaphor and Simile

In one line of a poem entitled *We are a People*, the writer mentions a "moccasin path." When readers see the word "moccasin," a picture may take shape in their minds, triggering an association with a specific group of people, Native Americans. Being able to create such mental pictures and form such associations will enable readers to more accurately interpret the other lines of the poem. In some writings, one picture like this may be the foundation for understanding the entire piece. In the poem *We Are a People,* the people group is never identified . . . except through the use of implied metaphors and images. Be sure to pay careful attention to titles and headings, where clue words often show up.

QUICK TIP:

Sometimes, one word or phrase may be the foundation for understanding an entire reading. Clue words often show up in titles or headings.

In a passage by Lewis Thomas, from *The Attic of the Brain*, Thomas helps the reader create a mental picture of an attic in an old house and then begins to describe how the brain has its own kind of "attic." An astute reader will begin to create her own images simply by reading a few words presented in an intriguing title. The brain does not have a physical "attic," but the metaphor enables the reader to draw relevant and enlightening comparisons. Such comparisons are sometimes signaled by such clue words as *like, as,* or *similar* to introduce a simile. For example, Thomas makes the following two direct comparisons, or similes, toward the end of his passage:

> *Attempting to operate one's own mind, powered by such a magical instrument as the human brain, strikes me as rather* like *using the world's biggest computer to add columns of figures, or towing a Rolls-Royce with a nylon rope.*

Here the human brain is compared to a magical instrument, and "attempting to operate" one's mind is compared to two other unlikely tasks.

Since similes are usually easier to recognize than metaphors, let's practice a few of those.

> A *quarrelsome wife is* like *a constant dripping on a rainy day.*

> (*Proverbs* 27:15)

What two things are being compared here? A quarrelsome wife and a constant dripping of rain. The writer is attempting to communicate some things about a quarrelsome wife using constant dripping as the "picture." What do you think of when you picture a constant dripping? While some people might actually enjoy the sound of rain, we know from the writer's choice of the word *quarrelsome* that he is creating a negative comparison. Use of the word *constant* implies something that might be repeated to the point of irritation. The reader may identify constant dripping as being tiresome, annoying, or even exasperating— not a glowing comparison for a quarrelsome wife.

Here's another simile:

> Like *clouds and wind without rain is a man who boasts of his gifts falsely.*
>
> (*Proverbs* 25:14)

In this verse, the gifts of a man who boasts falsely are compared to clouds and wind without rain. Since clouds and wind often result in rain, the picture of clouds and wind *without* rain helps the reader understand that a braggart's gifts may not live up to what is expected.

Now look at one more simile:

> *Some people view the commitment of marriage as an alligator from some murky swamp.*
>
> (Albom, 1997)

In this sentence, the commitment of marriage is compared to an alligator from a murky swamp. Let's first think of the pictures the word *alligator* calls up. Alligators might be seen as frightening and dangerous. In addition, a murky swamp could be described as dark or gloomy—a place you wouldn't want to enter. The reader gets the impression that some people see the commitment of marriage as something frightening, dangerous, and forbidding. Just as a murky swamp makes it hard to see what's ahead, it might be difficult for some to commit to a relationship when what will happen in the future is impossible to predict.

Here's one more sentence which combines a simile and a metaphor:

> *ALS is like a lit candle; it melts your nerves and leaves your body a pile of wax.*
>
> (Albom, 1997)

1. What is the simile? <u>ALS is like a lit candle</u>

2. What is the metaphor? <u>your body a pile of wax</u>

SIMILE/METAPHOR PRACTICE ONE:

The practice exercise below is taken from the following website:

http://volweb.utk.edu/Schools/bedford/harrisms/1poe.htm

First identify each sentence as a simile (s), or a metaphor (m), by writing the appropriate letter in the blank preceding each number. Remember that a simile is using words such as *like* or *as* to make a comparison between two things, while a metaphor makes a comparison between two things without using like or as.

_____   1. The baby was like an octopus, grabbing at all the cans on the grocery store shelves.

_____   2. As the teacher entered the room she muttered under her breath, "This class is like a three-ring circus!"

_____   3. The giant's steps were thunder as he ran toward Jack.

_____   4. The pillow was a cloud when I put my head upon it after a long day.

_____   5. I feel like a limp dishrag.

_____   6. Those girls are like two peas in a pod.

_____   7. The fluorescent light was the sun during our test.

_____   8. No one invites Harold to parties because he's a wet blanket.

_____   9. The bar of soap was a slippery eel during the dog's bath.

_____   10. Ted was as nervous as a cat with a long tail in a room full of rocking chairs.

Now go back through the ten sentences above, and in the blanks below, identify the two items being compared. The first one is done for you.

1. baby	octopus
2.	
3.	
4.	
5.	
6.	
7.	

8. _____

9. _____

10. _____

SIMILE/METAPHOR PRACTICE TWO:

The next practice on similes and metaphors lists expressions used in the novel _Tuesdays with Morrie_, by Mitch Albom. Identify each thought as a simile (s), or a metaphor (m), in the blanks below:

_____ 1. The newspaper had been _my lifeline, my oxygen._

_____ 2. He had created a _cocoon_ of human activities—conversation, interaction, affection . . .

_____ 3. . . . and it filled his life like an _overflowing soup bowl._

_____ 4. Morrie had become a _prisoner of his chair._

_____ 5. Sometimes he would close his eyes and try to draw the air up into his mouth and nostrils, and it seemed as if he were _trying to lift an anchor._

Now reread each thought above, and try to rewrite each underlined word or phrase in a more literal way on the lines below. The first one is done for you.

A. <u>something needed to live or to stay alive</u>

B. _____

C. _____

D. _____

E. _____

SIMILE/METAPHOR PRACTICE THREE:

The final practice on metaphors is a more challenging reading in which metaphors are implied, though not directly stated. Read the poem below and then answer the questions that follow.

Why I am Not a Painter

By Frank O'Hara

I am not a painter, I am a poet.
Why? I think I would rather be
a painter, but I am not. Well,

For instance, Mike Goldberg
is starting a painting. I drop in.
"Sit down and have a drink" he
says. I drink; we drink. I look
up. "You have SARDINES in it."
"Yes, it needed something there."
"Oh." I go and the days go by
and I drop in again. The painting
is going on, and I go, and the days
go by. I drop in. The painting is
finished. "Where's SARDINES?"
All that's left is just
letters, "It was too much," Mike says.

But me? One day I am thinking of
a color: orange. I write a line
about orange. Pretty soon it is a
whole page of words, not lines.
Then another page. There should be
so much more, not of orange, of
words, of how terrible orange is
and life. Days go by. It is even in
prose, I am a real poet. My poem
is finished and I haven't mentioned
orange yet. It's twelve poems, I call
it ORANGES. And one day in a gallery
I see Mike's painting, called SARDINES.

Some students understand the main point of this poem immediately, while others struggle. It's often a good idea to begin to bring meaning to a reading by starting with the title.

1. What do the title, and the poem, suggest about painting and poetry?

   _____

   _____

2. Are these art forms different or alike, or both?

   _____

   _____

3. What are some similarities and/or differences?

   _____

   _____

4. Is the tone of the writing more serious . . . or humorous?

   _____

   _____

5. Does the poet offer logical explanations for choosing writing over painting?

   _____

   _____

6. What is the most obvious implied metaphor in this poem?

   _____

   _____

7. Notice that the 12 poems are called *Oranges*, while the painting is called *Sardines*. How are these titles similar? How does this similarity relate to the main point of the poem?

   _____

   After answering the questions above, write a brief paragraph on the lines below, summarizing the poem:

   _____

   _____

   _____

   _____

   _____

   _____

B. Personification

Personification is a writing technique, which attributes human qualities to an object, animal, or idea. While this technique is often used in poetry and other forms of creative writing, it is also commonly used in other types of writing. For instance, when describing the music of Elvin Jones and John Coltrane, *Newsweek* had this to say:

> *Coltrane's saxophone was the soaring, often tormented soul; Jones's drums were the beating heart—and a constant storm of commentary and suggestion.*

Obviously, a saxophone is not a soul, much less a tormented one. Nor are drums a beating heart. However, music (or in this case, musical instruments) may help convey thoughts and feelings normally ascribed to people.

When personification is used, it may bring life and meaning to a description—much like a picture or video may "breathe life" (another example of personification) into the words on a page. The technique helps us, the readers, to form our own mental pictures based on prior knowledge or past experiences. Consider this line from Kahlil Gibran (1923):

> *But let there be spaces in your togetherness,*
> *And let the winds of the heavens dance between you.*

The first half of the thought is literal and clear, while the second half is poetic and helps us to "see" the truth of the literal half.

QUICK TIP:

As with other forms of figurative language, personification often helps the reader to form mental pictures based on prior knowledge or past experiences.

Now read the following passage from *20/20 Hindsight* by Jay Ford (1996), and answer the questions which follow.

> *In Kenya I felt more free than I have ever felt before. The only thing holding me captive was the earth which would grow the food, the sky which would quench*

*the earth of its thirst, and the sun which would warm and help all things to grow.
But these masters were sure to give back all that you have put in.*

What three objects were holding the writer *captive?*

1. Earth
2. Sky
3. Sun

What are your thoughts on how these objects might hold someone captive, and why does the writer call them *masters?*

*Though answers may vary, you might have considered the need for these aspects
of nature in order for one to live.*

PERSONIFICATION PRACTICE:

The following sentences were used in a business article entitled "Quitting Time" (*Newsweek*, 2004). Underline each specific example of personification below and then identify their meanings in your own words.

*Or maybe we'll catch a glimpse of that telltale stationery peeking out from his
desk—the heavy, ivory stock that's a give-away he's been printing resumes.*

_____

_____

Companies hired briskly in March and April, and economists predict the unemployment rate will continue its steady downward march.

_____

_____

*That's largely because companies spent the past few years squeezing more and
more work out of ever-smaller staffs, and many workers aren't happy about it.*

_____

_____

*We're still a long way from the days when every worker bee felt like the king of
the jungle. But in the months ahead, there's hope of hearing at least a few roars.*

_____

_____

C. Hyperbole

A hyperbole (pronounced hy-pēr-bò-lē) is a deliberate overstatement or exaggeration.

Examples of Common Types of Hyperbole

He was *scared to death.*

Don't go out without a coat; you'll *catch your death* (of cold).

I'm so hungry, *I could eat a horse.*

We're *starving!*

She's *as big as a house.*

I've told you *a thousand times* to pick up those toys!

I thought that sermon would last *forever!*

In the 1982 book, *And More by Andy Rooney*, Andrew A. Rooney (humorous speaker/writer) includes a chapter entitled "Living is Dangerous to Your Health." The title and chapter are both exaggerations meant to make fun of the constant bombardment of news indicating how many things are bad for us. Hyperbole is often used to provide humor or special effect. The overstatement makes an impression on the reader.

QUICK TIP:

As with other forms of figurative language, hyperbole is not meant to be taken literally. The overstatement or exaggeration is used to make an impression on the reader. It may provide humor or some other special effect. Ask yourself what effect the writer may be trying to produce.

You may have seen or heard the common phrase, "blazing inferno." According to writer and lexicographer, Betty Kirkpatrick (*Clichés*, 1996), the phrase is used often by journalists in headlines such as "man leaps from roof in blazing inferno." Kirkpatrick asserts that the term would "properly be used to describe a very large and dangerous fire, but is in fact often used to describe anything bigger than a small garden rubbish fire, the tabloid press having a weakness for exaggeration, which sells more copies of newspapers."

A recent political cartoon (*Non Sequitur* by Wiley, 2004), criticized both major political parties by labeling an office the "Center For The Obfuscation, Distortion And *Hyperbolizing* of Reality Beyond Recognition" and calling it "The Most Bi-Partisan Organization in the Country." In other words, according to the cartoonist, political parties tend to make vague, distorted, or exaggerated statements for political gain.

Not all hyperboles, however, receive such negative commentary. Take the following well known stanza from Ralph Waldo Emerson's *Concord Hymn*, written for the dedication of the Obelisk, a battle monument commemorating the valiant efforts put forth by area citizens on April 19, 1775:

> *By the rude bridge that arched the flood,*
> *Their flag to April's breeze unfurled;*
> *Here once the embattled farmers stood;*
> *And <u>fired the shot heard round the world</u>.*

Given that a shot could not be heard *round the world*, how would you interpret the hyperbole underlined in the above stanza?

_____

_____

_____

_____

Did your answer include the idea that the shot had far-reaching consequences or interest? If so, you're on the right track! Great!

HYPERBOLE PRACTICE

Now write a more literal alternative for each of the hyberboles underlined below:

1. He made *a ton of money* in the stock market.

_____

2. He has *a million relatives.*

_____

3. *Her beauty could move mountains.*

---

4. *She is a giant in this industry.*

---

5. *His mouth could rival the Grand Canyon.*

One last challenging example and description of hyperbole is taken from the following website:

http://www.uncp.edu/home/canada/work/allam/general/glossary.htm

> *In poetry, hyperbole can emphasize or dramatize a person's opinions or emotions. Skilled poets use hyperbole to describe intense emotions and mental states. Othello uses hyperbole to describe his anger at the possibility of Iago lying about his wife's infidelity in Act III, Scene III of Shakespeare's play* Othello:
>
> > If thou dost slander her and torture me,
> > Never pray more; abandon all remorse;
> > On horror's head accumulate;
> > Do deeds to make heaven weep, all earth amazed;
> > For nothing canst thou to damnation add
> > Greater than that.
>
> *In this passage, Othello is telling Iago that if he is lying then Othello will have no pity and Iago will have no hope for salvation. Adding horrors with still more horrors, Othello is describing his potential rage. Othello even declares that the Earth will be confounded with horror at Othello's actions in such a state of madness.*
>
> (*A Glossary of Literary Terms, A Handbook to Literature*. Andy Stamper, Student, University of North Carolina at Pembroke)

CHAPTER SUMMARY

- **FIGURATIVE LANGUAGE:** Frequently used in poetry and other types of literature, but may show up in any kind of writing. It is not to be taken literally, but is used to add interest and stimulate the imagination. While knowing the specific terms for common forms of figurative language may not be necessary, the reader's awareness and recognition of these forms should help create mental pictures that bring meaning and depth to a reading.

- **METAPHOR:** Draws comparisons between two things without using words such as *like*, *as*, or *similar*. These also help the reader to see how things are alike, but may be more challenging to recognize or interpret than similes, since the comparison word clues are not directly stated.

- **SIMILE:** Draws comparisons between two things, using words such as *like*, *as*, or *similar*. These help the reader to see how things are alike. One word or phrase may sometimes provide the foundation for understanding an entire reading. Pay special attention to titles and headings.

- **PERSONIFICATION:** Attributes human qualities to an object, animal, or idea. As with other types of figurative language, personification may bring life and meaning to a description and help readers to form mental pictures based on prior knowledge or past experiences.

- **HYPERBOLE:** A deliberate overstatement or exaggeration. As with other forms of figurative language, hyperbole is not meant to be taken literally. The exaggeration is used to make an impression on the reader. It may provide humor or some other special effect. Ask yourself what effect the writer may be trying to produce.

QUICK CONNECTIONS—CHAPTER FIVE

News Source Connection

Using a news source (news magazine or newspaper), skim the source, looking for examples of the four types of figurative language covered in this chapter. Find and mark (or list) at least two examples of each. Then identify how each example could be stated in a literal way.

Textbook Connection

Some textbooks lend themselves more to locating figurative language than others. If you're reading a textbook for another course, and the text does incorporate figurative language, write the title of the text and then list at least four figurative expressions you are able to find. Also write a short response, explaining why that subject area might lend itself to expressions of figurative language. If you have a textbook for another course, that does not incorporate figurative language, write a brief response explaining why literal language is more appropriate for that text. Then list at least five general courses that probably would use textbooks which incorporate figurative language.

Novel Connection

Using a course novel, or any novel acceptable to your instructor, skim for examples of the four types of figurative language covered in this chapter. Try to find at least two examples of each. Then prepare a matching game for another student in the course by folding a clean sheet of paper into eighths and writing one example (you've found) on each section. On a separate sheet of paper, also folded into eight sections, restate each example in a literal way. Number each section on both sheets so that the matches have the same numbers. Then cut each sheet, clipping all the figurative expressions together and all the literal restatements together. You will have two separate piles. Be sure they are scrambled, so that they are ready to be matched by another student.

Computer Connection

Using Google or another search engine, type *figurative language* in the search bar. Find sites that end with *edu* and that are also connected with a university or college. Search until you find at least four types of figurative language that are not included in this chapter. List the four types you found, and at least one example of each. At the bottom of your paper, be sure to identify the sites you used as well.

Patterns
of Organization
Strategies

Chapter Preview

Patterns of Organization Strategies Overview

A. Narration

B. Description

C. Process Analysis

D. Classification

E. Comparison/Contrast

F. Cause and Effect

G. Definition

A writer uses patterns to organize writing
         a reader must use them to organize reading

Objectives

- Student will be able to recognize different patterns of organization.
- Student will be able to identify the organization within each pattern.
- Student will be able to analyze information from each pattern.
- Student will understand the purpose of each pattern.

Readiness Quiz

Section 1: Match the following terms on the left with the definitions on the right.

1. Narration	A. to explain or analyze reasons, results, or both
2. Description	B. to explain parts, or to sort into categories
3. Process Analysis	C. to relate an event or a series of events
4. Classification	D. to define a term or clarify the meaning
5. Comparison/Contrast	E. to explain how to do something
6. Cause and Effect	F. to create a vivid mental picture
7. Definition	G. to show how things are alike and different

Readiness Quiz

Section 2: Match the following statements on the left with the terms on the right.

1. The first thing you need to do to organize your closet is to get some shelves. Second, you need some boxes and pens for labeling.	A. Description
2. Feng shui is the ancient Chinese art of harmony and balance.	B. Narration
3. That lady shot him because he stole her purse.	C. Classification
4. My wedding day was the most exciting day of my life!	D. Comparison/Contrast
5. Movies have various genres such as horror, comedy, romance, or drama.	E. Cause and Effect
6. The dark, sleek shark moves effortlessly through the misty-blue water.	F. Definition
7. Country music and rock 'n roll are alike in some ways, but they can be very different.	G. Process Analysis

Patterns of Organization Strategies Overview

Why does a reader need to understand the author's pattern of organization? A pattern of organization refers to how a paragraph's sentences are structured or arranged. Understanding how to recognize the different patterns improves your reading comprehension. When authors write, they choose a structure or style that fits the topic. As readers begin to recognize the various patterns, relationships among ideas become clearer. This clarity improves comprehension because the reader is better able to follow the development of an idea from start to finish. When reading, look for the controlling idea, a word or thought that is repeated within the passage. The sentences of a paragraph are said to be *united* when they work together to support the main idea.

Readers should ask the following questions when reading:

1. How are the author's details organized? Is he or she telling a story, describing something, showing a process?

2. What unifies or ties together the author's writing? Are key words or ideas repeated, and/or are transitional words used?

Writers often mix patterns in their writings. This approach provides the reader with various ways to understand the subject. For example, the subject may first be described and then a story may follow. Being aware of these patterns enables the reader to make more connections among the details and improves comprehension.

This chapter addresses the following seven patterns of organization:

1. Narration
2. Description
3. Process Analysis
4. Classification
5. Comparison/Contrast
6. Cause and Effect
7. Definition

Purpose of Organizational Patterns

Pattern	Purpose
Narration	To relate an event or series of events leading to an outcome
Description	To create a vivid mental picture
Process Analysis	To explain how to do something or how something occurs
Classification	To explain parts of a whole or to sort into categories or groups
Comparison/Contrast	To tell how two things are similar or different, or both
Cause and Effect	To explain and/or analyze reasons, results, or both
Definition	To define a term, either to clarify its meaning or to suggest a new meaning

Important Aspects of Each Organizational Pattern

Pattern	Important Aspects
Narration	Story, told in first or third person; tells who, what, why, when, where, and how; sequence of events is important. **Transition words (after, later, during, never, suddenly, last)**
Description	Details that appeal to the five senses and create a visualization for the reader. **Transitions words (for example, such as)**
Process Analysis	Describes a method of doing something; sequence is extremely important; look for steps and order. **Transition words (first, next, after, before, following, stage, secondly)**

Pattern	*Important Aspects*
Classification	Divides a subject into various parts or identifies a member of a group based on similar characteristics; look for part-to-whole relationship or various categories into which a large number of things can be sorted. **Transition words (part, type, group, category, class, member)**
Comparison/ Contrast	Shows how two things are alike or different. Can be organized subject by subject, or point by point. **Transition words (in comparison, similarly, like, in contrast, on the other hand, whereas)**
Cause and Effect	Causes are reasons behind an event (reasons that explain how or why); effects are results of events (which explain what happened or the end result). **Transition words (reason, result, thus, since, therefore, consequently, due to)**
Definition	Defines a person, place, thing or idea by explaining the characteristics that distinguish it from others in its class. **Transitions words (for example, to illustrate, such as, means, is defined, can be seen as)**

Transition Words

Transitions are words or phrases that allow the reader to follow a writer's ideas. They assist in *bridging* or connecting the ideas in a passage and create a sense of unity. To learn more about important transitions that can help you verify the pattern of organization the author has chosen, refer to the previous charts. They summarize the purposes and important aspects of each pattern, along with the transition words that can help you identify them.

QUICK TIP:

Transition words create a powerful link between ideas in a writing. Think of them as a bridge.

The best way to learn to recognize patterns of organization is by reading and practicing. The following pages provide examples of each of the patterns. Read the examples and answer the questions that follow. Make sure you do not skip the Preparing to Read introductions, which will guide your understanding of each pattern.

A. Narration

Preparing to Read

Can you recall a time in your life when you had an experience that changed something you believed? In *Salvation*, Langston Hughes shares his experience of being saved. As you read, notice that it is a retelling of a specific event. Notice the relevance of the sequence of events in understanding the progression, or how one thing leads to another. Look for transition words and phrases.

SALVATION

Langston Hughes

I was saved from sin when I was going on thirteen. But not really saved. It happened like this. There was a big revival at my Auntie Reed's church. Every night for weeks there had been much preaching, singing, praying, and shouting, and some very hardened sinners had been brought to Christ, and the membership of the church had grown by leaps and bounds. Then just before the revival ended, they held a special meeting for children, "to bring the young lambs to the fold." My aunt spoke of it for days ahead. That night I was escorted to the front row and placed on the mourners' bench with all the other young sinners, who had not yet been brought to Jesus.

My aunt told me that when you were saved you saw a light, and something happened to you inside! And Jesus came into your life! And God was with you from then on! She said you could see and hear and feel Jesus in your soul. I believed her. I had heard a great many old people say the same thing and it seemed to me they ought to know. So I sat there calmly in the hot, crowded church, waiting for Jesus to come to me.

The preacher preached a wonderful rhythmical sermon, all moans and shouts and lonely cries and dire pictures of hell, and then he sang a song about the ninety and nine safe in the fold, but one little lamb was left out in the cold. Then he said: "Won't you come? Won't you come to Jesus? Young lambs, won't you come?" And he held out his arms to all us young sinners there on the mourners' bench. And the little girls

Source: *Strategies for College Writing*, Prentice Hall, 2003.

cried. And some of them jumped up and went to Jesus right away. But most of us just sat there.

A great many old people came and knelt around us and prayed, old women with jet-black faces and braided hair, old men with work-gnarled hands. And the church sang a song about the lower lights are burning, some poor sinners to be saved. And the whole building rocked with prayer and song.

Still I kept waiting to *see* Jesus.

Finally all the young people had gone to the altar and were saved, but one boy and me. He was a rounder's son named Westley. Westley and I were surrounded by sisters and deacons praying. It was very hot in the church, and getting late now. Finally Westley said to me in a whisper: "God damn! I'm tired o' sitting here. Let's get up and be saved." So he got up and was saved.

Then I was left all alone on the mourners' bench. My aunt came and knelt at my knees and cried, while prayers and song swirled all around me in the little church. The whole congregation prayed for me alone, in a mighty wail of moans and voices. And I kept waiting serenely for Jesus, waiting, waiting—but he didn't come. I wanted to see him, but nothing happened to me. Nothing! I wanted something to happen to me, but nothing happened.

I heard the songs and the minister saying: "Why don't you come? My dear child, why don't you come to Jesus? Jesus is waiting for you. He wants you. Why don't you come? Sister Reed, what is this child's name?"

"Langston," my aunt sobbed.

"Langston, why don't you come? Why don't you come and be saved? Oh, Lamb of God! Why don't you come?"

Now it was really getting late. I began to be ashamed of myself, holding everything up so long. I began to wonder what God thought about Westley, who certainly hadn't seen Jesus either, but who was now sitting proudly on the platform, swinging his knickerbockered legs and grinning down at me, surrounded by deacons and old women on their knees praying. God had not struck Westley dead for taking his name in vain or for lying in the temple. So I decided that maybe to save further trouble, I'd better lie, too, and say that Jesus had come, and get up and be saved.

So I got up.

Suddenly the whole room broke into a sea of shouting, as they saw me rise. Waves of rejoicing swept the place. Women leaped in the air. My aunt threw her arms around me. The minister took me by the hand and led me to the platform.

When things quieted down, in a hushed silence, punctuated by a few ecstatic "Amens," all the new young lambs were blessed in the name of God. Then joyous singing filled the room.

That night, for the first time in my life (but one, for I was a big boy twelve years old)—I cried. I cried, in bed alone, and couldn't stop. I buried my head under the quilts, but my aunt heard me. She woke up and told my uncle I was crying because the Holy Ghost had come into my life, and because I had seen Jesus. But I was really crying because I couldn't bear to tell her that I had lied, that I had deceived everybody in the church, that I hadn't seen Jesus, and that now I didn't believe there was a Jesus anymore, since he didn't come to help me.

Questions

1. Who is the reading about? _____

2. What was Langston's purpose for writing this essay?

_____

_____

3. Can you make a short list of the sequence of events?

_____

_____

_____

_____

4. What transition words did you notice? ————————————

_____

_____

B. Description

Preparing to Read

Have you ever had the opportunity to see ocean life up close? In *The Great Tide Pool*, John Steinbeck *shows* with words what ocean life looks like. As you read, look for words and phrases that evoke the five senses.

THE GREAT TIDE POOL

John Steinbeck

Doc was collecting marine animals in the Great Tide Pool on the tip of the Peninsula. It is a fabulous place: when the tide is in, a wave-churned basin, creamy with foam, whipped by the combers that roll in from the whistling buoy on the reef. But when the tide goes out the little water

Source: *A Writer's Workshop* McGraw-Hill, 2002.

world becomes quiet and lovely. The sea is very clear and the bottom becomes fantastic with hurrying, fighting, feeding, breeding animals. Crabs rush from frond to frond of the waving algae. Starfish squat over mussels and limpets, attach their million little suckers and then slowly lift with incredible power until the prey is broken from the rock. And then the starfish stomach comes out and envelops its food. Orange and speckled and fluted nudibranches slide gracefully over the rocks, their skirts waving like the dresses of Spanish dancers. And black eels poke their heads out of crevices and wait for prey. The snapping shrimps with their trigger claws pop loudly. The lovely colored world is glassed over. Hermit crabs like frantic children scamper on the bottom sand. And now one, finding an empty snail shell he likes better than his own, creeps out, exposing his soft body to the enemy for a moment, and then pops into the new shell. A wave breaks over the barrier, and churns the glassy water for a moment and mixes bubbles into the pool, and then it clears and is tranquil and lovely and murderous again. Here a crab tears a leg from his brother. The anemones expand like soft and brilliant flowers, inviting any tired and perplexed animal to lie for a moment in their arms, and when some small crab of little tide-pool Johnnie accepts the green and purple invitation, the petals whip in, the stinging cells shoot tiny narcotic needles into the prey and it grows weak and perhaps sleepy while the searing caustic digestive acids melt its body down.

Then the creeping murderer, the octopus, steals out, slowly, softly, moving like a gray mist, pretending now to be a bit of weed, now a rock, now a lump of decaying meat while its evil goat eyes watch coldly. It oozes and flows toward a feeding crab, and as it comes close its yellow eyes burn and its body turns rosy with the pulsing color of anticipating and rage. Then suddenly it runs lightly on the tips of its arms as ferociously as a charging cat. It leaps savagely on the crab, there is a puff of black fluid, and the struggling mass is obscured in the sepia cloud while the octopus murders the crab. On the exposed rocks out of water, the barnacles bubble behind their closed doors and the limpets dry out. And down to the rocks come the black flies to eat anything they can find. The sharp smell of iodine from the algae, and the lime smell of calcareous bodies and the smell of powerful protean, smell of sperm and ova fill the air. On the exposed rocks the starfish emit semen and eggs from between their rays. The smells of life and richness, of death and digestion, of decay and birth, burden the air. And salt spray blows in from the barrier where the ocean waits for its rising-tide strength to permit it back into the Great Tide Pool again. And on the reef the whistling buoys sit like a sad and patient bull.

Questions

1. Fill in the chart below with words and phrases that appeal to your senses.

Taste	Touch	Smell	Hear	See%

2. What transition words did you notice?

C. Process Analysis

Preparing to Read

Have you ever thought about the steps involved in writing a letter? As you read, notice how Garrison Keillor lays out these steps within his essay.

HOW TO WRITE A LETTER

Garrison Keillor

We shy persons need to write a letter now and then, or else we'll dry up and blow away. It's true. And I speak as one who loves to reach for the phone, dial the number, and talk. I say, "Big Bopper here—what's shakin', babes?" The telephone is to shyness what Hawaii is to February, it's a way out of the woods, *and yet*: a letter is better.

   Such a sweet gift—a piece of handmade writing, in an envelope that is not a bill, sitting in our friend's path when she trudges home from

Source: *A Writer's Workshop* McGraw-Hill, 2002.

a long day spent among wahoos and savages, a day our words will help repair. They don't need to be immortal, just sincere. She can read them twice and again tomorrow. *You're someone I care about, Corrine, and think of often and every time I do you make me smile.*

We need to write, otherwise nobody will know who we are. They will have only a vague impression of us as A Nice Person, because, frankly, we don't shine at conversation, we lack the confidence to thrust our faces forward and say, "Hi, I'm Heather Hooten; let me tell you about my week." Mostly we say "Uh-huh" and "Oh, really." People smile and look over our shoulder, looking for someone else to meet.

So a shy person sits down and writes a letter. To be known by another person—to meet and talk freely on the page—to be close despite distance. To escape from anonymity and be our own sweet selves and express the must of our souls.

Same thing that moves a giant rock star to sing his heart out in front of 123,000 people moves us to take ballpoint in hand and write a few lines to our dear Aunt Eleanor. *We want to be known.* We want her to know that we have fallen in love, that we quit our job, that we're moving to New York, and we want to say a few things that might not get said in casual conversation: *Thank you for what you've meant to me, I am very happy right now.*

The first step in writing letters is to get over the guilt of *not* writing. You don't "owe" anybody a letter. Letters are a gift. The burning shame you feel when you see unanswered mail makes it harder to pick up a pen and makes for a cheerless letter when you finally do. *I feel bad about not writing, but I've been so busy, etc.* Skip this. Few letters are obligatory, and they are *Thanks for the wonderful gift* and *I am terribly sorry to hear about George's death* and *Yes, you're welcome to stay with us next month,* and not many more than that. Write those promptly if you want to keep your friends. Don't worry about the others, except love letters, of course. When your true love writes, *Dear Light of My Life, Joy of My Heart, O Lovely Pulsating Core of My Sensate Life,* some response is called for.

Some of the best letters are tossed off in a burst of inspiration, so keep your writing stuff in one place where you can sit down for a few minutes and (*Dear Roy, I am in the middle of a book entitled* We Are Still Married *but thought I'd drop you a line. Hi to your sweetie, too*) dash off a note to a pal. Envelopes, stamps, address book, everything in a drawer so you can write fast when the pen is hot.

A blank white eight-by-eleven sheet can look as big as Montana if the pen's not so hot—try a smaller page and write boldly. Or use a note card with a piece of fine art on the front; if your letter ain't good, at least they get the Matisse. Get a pen that makes a sensuous line, get a comfortable typewriter, a friendly word processor—whichever feels easy to the hand.

Sit for a few minutes with the blank sheet in front of you, and meditate on the person you will write to, let your friend come to mind until you can almost see her or him in the room with you. Remember the last time you saw each other and how your friend looked and what you said and what perhaps was unsaid between you, and when your friend becomes real to you, start to write.

Write the salutation—*Dear You*—and take a deep breath and plunge in. A simple declarative sentence will do, followed by another and another and another. Tell us what you're doing and tell it like you were talking to us. Don't think about grammar, don't think about lit'ry style, don't try to write dramatically, just give us your news. Where did you go, who did you see, what did they say, what do you think?

If you don't know where to begin, start with the present moment: *I'm sitting at the kitchen table on a rainy Saturday morning. Everyone is gone and the house is quiet.* Let your simple description of the present moment lead to something else, let the letter drift gently along.

The toughest letter to crank out is one that is meant to impress, as we all know from writing job applications; if it's hard work to slip off a letter to a friend, maybe you're trying too hard to be terrific. A letter is only a report to someone who already likes you for reasons other than your brilliance. Take it easy.

Don't worry about form. It's not a term paper. When you come to the end of one episode, just start a new paragraph. You can go from a few lines about the sad state of pro football to the fight with your mother to your fond memories of Mexico to your cat's urinary-tract infection to a few thoughts on personal indebtedness and on to the kitchen sink and what's in it. The more you write, the easier it gets, and when you have a True Friend to write to, a *compadre*, a soul sibling, then it's like driving a car down a country road, you just get behind the keyboard and press on the gas.

Don't tear up the page and start over when you write a bad line—try to write your way out of it. Make mistakes and plunge on. Let the letter cook along and let yourself be bold. Outrage, confusion, love—whatever is in your mind, let it find a way to the page. Writing is a means of discovery, always, and when you come to the end and write *Yours ever* or *Hugs and kisses*, you'll know something you didn't when you wrote *Dear Pal*.

Probably your friend will put your letter away, and it'll be read again a few years from now—and it will improve with age. And forty years from now, your friend's grandkids will dig it out of the attic and read it, a sweet and precious relic of the ancient eighties that gives them a sudden clear glimpse of you and her and the world we old-timers knew. You will then have created an object of art. Your simple lines about where you went, who you saw, what they said, will speak to those children and they will feel in their hearts the humanity of our times.

You can't pick up a phone and call the future and tell them about our times. You have to pick up a piece of paper.

Questions

1. According to the author, what are the steps in writing a letter?

Step 1: _____

Step 2: _____

Step 3: _____

Step 4: _____

Step 5: _____

Step 6: _____

2. Why is the sequence of the reading so important?

_____

3. What transition words did you notice?

_____

D. Classification

Preparing to Read

Think of any topic and how you would break it down into *categories*. The following article is divided into categories of family violence. As you read, notice that the format is similar to that of a textbook.

FAMILY VIOLENCE: WHY WE HURT THE ONES WE LOVE

Sandra Arbetter

When the lake waters swirled over the car holding Susan Smith's two little boys, the ripple was felt around the nation. How could the sweet-looking mother from the peaceful town of Union, South Carolina, drown her own children? Wake up, America. There are 600 cases every year of mothers killing their children, according to the U.S. Department of

Source: *Building Strategies for College Reading* Prentice Hall, 2001.

Justice. The Smith case jolted folks out of the numbness created by daily headlines of beatings, rapes, shootings, stabbings, and torture—all in the family. Maybe it was the news photos of the two handsome little faces. Maybe it was the murders coming so soon after O. J. Simpson was charged with stabbing to death his ex-wife, Nicole, and her friend Ron Goldman. How could a national sports hero be associated with such messy business as spousal abuse and murder?

The facts about family violence are coming out of the closet, and they reveal that children and wives are not the only family members mistreated. The web of family violence entangles husbands abused by wives and sisters abused by each other.

The statistics on family violence are staggering: Every 15 seconds a woman in this county is battered. Almost 2 million women are severely assaulted every year. One-third of female homicide victims are killed by a husband or partner.

Spousal abuse occurs in families of every racial, ethnic, and economic group. In a recent study at the University of Rhode Island, for example, nearly 20 of every 1000 women with family incomes over $40,000 reported being victims of severe violence. Last year more than 1 million teens ran away from home. Most left, not for the excitement of the streets or to be grown-up, but to escape beatings and sexual abuse and worse at home. One in 25 elderly persons is victimized. Almost one-third of the maltreatment is by adult children of the elderly, according to the U.S. Department of Health and Human Services. Three million cases of child abuse or neglect were reported in 1994. About half involve neglect, which means that adults are not providing a safe environment with adequate shelter, clothing, food, and sanitation. Abuse includes physical or emotional injury or sexual abuse.

Effects on Victims

But the numbers don't tell the whole story. It's the suffering of each victim that matters most. "I can't trust anyone," says 21-year-old Dan. "I feel lonely all the time." When the people who are supposed to take care of you are hurting you instead, then nothing is safe. It can be hard to get along with friends and co-workers, or to have a long-term intimate relationship.

Children who witness (or are victims of) abuse are at risk for school problems, drug abuse, sexual acting out, running away, suicide, and becoming abusers themselves. Their self-esteem is shattered by feelings of powerlessness to protect themselves or the parent who is being abused.

Girls from abusive homes tend to become victims. Boys tend to see violence as the way to deal with frustration.

Children from abusive families learn a false lesson: Love and violence go together. The person who loves you hits you, so you hit the person you love.

An Old Story

The violence is nothing new, but until recently there was an unwritten conspiracy to ignore it. Americans wanted to hold on to the image that families were all sweetness and light. When there was abuse, often a husband beating a wife, it was dismissed with a knowing smile as part of being in love.

Sweetness and light? Tell that to the 3.3 million children between the ages of 3 and 17 who are at risk from parental violence, according to Peter Jaffe, author of *Children of Abused Women*. Tell that to the thousands of children who have been wrenched from their abusive home to live in shelters or foster care. . . . .

Why Men Abuse

More than 90 percent of the reported battering is done by the male partner, although the whole story of abuse by women is yet to be told. The shame of it keeps many men from reporting it, according to experts; men abuse by:

Physical abuse

Emotional abuse

Economic abuse (taking her money, making her ask for money)

Sexual abuse (making her do things against her will)

Isolation (controlling her activities, who she sees, who she talks to)

What causes men to abuse women they say they love? Experts say it has a lot to do with feelings of powerlessness. A man who abuses may look tough on the outside, but he often has low self-esteem and is very dependent on the woman. He expects her to meet all his needs. Solve his loneliness; make him feel good about himself. If she wants to go out with friends or make some decisions of her own, he feels abandoned. Violence steps in to keep the woman fearful of going against his wishes. The man often puts down his partner, calling her dumb or ugly or useless. Heard often enough, that wears down the woman's self-esteem so that she questions her ability to leave and make it on her own. . . . .

Child Abuse

Every day in this country, children are killed by parents and caretakers. Men more than women tend to shake babies to stop them from crying, according to a report from the U.S. Advisory Board on Child Abuse and Neglect. This can cause death: Neck muscles are not fully developed; the baby's head moves violently; the brain is pulled different directions, and brain cells tear. The problem is how to get untrained parents to understand that babies do not cry to irritate their mothers and fathers. Their crying communicates some need, and they can't stop just because someone is angry at the noise.

Women kill most often through severe neglect—like the mother in Memphis who left two toddlers in the car last June in 90-degree heat while she partied with friends. Temperatures in the car soared, and the children died.

Now statistics show an increase in the rate of abuse of adolescents. Teen abuse has been underreported, possibly because adults see teens as able to protect themselves. . . . .

Elder Abuse

Grandparents are for hugs and I-Love-You drawings and visits on holidays. But did you know that some are abused? The elderly who are abused are often too frail to defend themselves and too ashamed to report mistreatment. Dr. David Finkelhor of the University of New Hampshire has identified three kinds of elder abuse:

Psychological abuse (name calling, insulting, ignoring, threatening)

Financial abuse (illegal or unethical use of the elderly person's funds)

Physical abuse (hitting, pushing, confining, sexual abuse)

Most elderly are abused by those they live with—partly the result of the stress of caring for a person who is ill or disabled, who needs to be fed and toileted, and who provides little satisfying companionship. Abusers usually have a history of substance abuse or mental illness. Two-thirds of them are financially dependent on the victim. There can even be an element of the adult child "getting even" for past abuse by the parent. . . . .

Between Brothers and Sisters

If we have ignored spousal and elder abuse, we have all but denied the existence of sibling abuse, which often is chalked up to normal sibling rivalry. "I begged my parents not to go out and let my sister, Lila, baby-sit," said Sam, now 17. "She'd sit on me and put a pillow over my face and punch my head. She'd tickle me until I wet my pants, and then threaten to tell everyone at school about it. Once she pointed my father's gun at me and said she'd kill me if I didn't do what she asked."

Sam's mother and father thought his complaints were just childish squabbles between brother and sister. It turned out that Lila's behavior was a call for help. When Sam got a concussion after Lila tripped him, the whole family went for counseling. As they all learned to communicate their feelings verbally and to express praise and appreciation of one another, Lila's abusive behavior lessened . . . .

Getting Help

If you are being abused, tell someone. Some people are afraid to tell for fear they'll be sent away, the family will be torn apart, or that other family members will be angry. But what is the alternative—to continue to live with an abuser, to have your self-esteem plunge to zero, to risk getting into trouble, to be badly injured? . . . .

Of course, many children from abusive homes go on to have successful lives with loving relationships. While some studies say 80 percent of abusers were abused as children, other research puts the figure closer to 30 percent. While that is still higher than the base rate of 5 percent for abuse in the general population, it means that up to 70 percent of children who were abused do not grow up to be abusive to their family members.

In many ways, family violence remains a terrible puzzle. But now that personal histories are being made public and problems are being recognized as such, we have a chance to put some of the pieces together.

Questions

1. What are the categories of the subject "Family Violence?"

   _____

   _____

   _____

   _____

2. What are the characteristics of the following?

   Child Abuse

   _____

   _____

_____

_____

Men Who Abuse

_____

_____

_____

_____

3. What transition words did you notice?

_____

E. Comparison/Contrast

Preparing to Read

Compare (same) and contrast (different) readings show how two or more subjects are the same and how they differ. As you read, look for the difference between the family of the kids of the author's generation and the family of the kids from television shows such as _The Brady Bunch_ and other families from TV.

THEY STOLE OUR CHILDHOOD

Lee Goldberg

We're the wonderful generation.

We are the kids who were "so adult" when our divorced parents readjusted to the rigors of being suddenly single. We are the kids who discovered sex so early in our lives and were such overachievers in school.

We are looked on by our elders with admiration and awe. And yet, if you wipe away the surface gloss, you will find that we are actually victims, causalities of our parents' need for us to grow up fast. That which we are praised for is our biggest problem.

Day-to-day family life for us was a contradiction between what we saw on the _Brady Bunch_ and _Courtship of Eddie's Father_ and what we were actually living. We were supposed to be thinking about the big dance, playing baseball, getting new handlebars on our bikes, gossiping about our favorite TV stars and, when our parents weren't around, dressing up in their clothes and looking at ourselves in the mirror.

Source: _Writing Talk_ Prentice Hall, 2003.

Instead we found ourselves not only dressing up in their clothes, but adopting their state of mind as well. We worried about whether mom would receive her child-support check, whether our parent's date for tonight would become a breakfast guest tomorrow, whether our little sister would ever remember what it was like to have two parents under one roof.

Our parents were always so proud of our capacity to make it on our own, to "be adult." Parents were thinking of us less like children and more like peers. Suddenly we kids weren't being treated like kids anymore.

Part of being adult was not indulging the child in us that hungered for affections. Our generation, it seems, turned to sex for the affections we lacked at home. As we saw it, needing a hug wasn't very adult. Sleeping with someone was. It was an acceptable way to ask for the physical affirmation of self-worth that we weren't getting from our parents, who we saw doing little hugging and a lot of sleeping around.

We found that spending more time at school or work was a welcome alternative to going home in the afternoons. The media had taught us that coming home from school meant milk and cookies, TV and playing with friends, mom or a babysitter in the kitchen and dad back from work at 6. Suddenly, going home meant confronting dad's new girlfriend, mom's unpaid bills or playing parent to our younger siblings and our parents, too.

It's no wonder so many of us, barely into our '20s, feel as though we've already been married and raised children. In divorce, parents seem to become teen-agers, and the kids become the adults. Many of our younger brothers and sisters see us more as their parents than their real parents. As our parents pursued careers and re-entered the dating scene, we children coped by forming our own little mini-families, with the older kids parenting for the younger siblings. It was common for single mothers to joke about how eldest son played doting father, checking out her dates, offering sage advice. Or for parents to find their younger kids wouldn't accept candy from strangers unless an older sister OK'd it first.

Our parents expected us to understand their problems and frustrations, to grasp the complex machinations of divorce proceedings and the emotional hazards they faced by dating again. More than understanding. Our parents sometimes pressured us into becoming participants in their divorce proceedings, encouraging us to take sides. We found ourselves having to withdraw from them just to protect ourselves from the potential pain that could be caused by mixed parental loyalties in the midst of courtroom warfare.

We were rewarded with approval: "My kids are so grown-up," "my kids can handle things," "my kids coped so well," "my kids can make it on their own," "my kids are so together." What we missed was a chance to be childish, immature, and unafraid to admit we didn't have it all together.

We pay the price when we need parents to turn to and don't have them—as we toil with our first serious relationships and when our long-suppressed childish side rears its playful head.

Divorce didn't just split up our parents. It stole our childhood.

Our parents are paying, too. They ache for the closeness with us they never had and may never get. They try to grasp memories of our childhood and come up nearly empty. They find themselves separated from their children and wonder how the gap appeared. Some wake up to realize that they know their gas station attendant better than their children.

The cure is not to curb divorce. We can start by realizing that this generation, which may have it together intellectually, paid with its adolescence. What needs rethinking are the attitudes and expectations of parents. Kids who are mature are fine. Kids who are "so adult" need help.

Questions

1. What are the kids from the author's generation thinking about and/or doing according to the author?
2. What are the kids of the television families thinking about and/or doing according to the author?
3. What are similarities between the two groups?

F. Cause and Effect

Preparing to Read

Why do you think that Americans like horror movies? As you read, notice the cause–effect relationship Steven King provides between horror movies and sanity.

WHY WE CRAVE HORROR MOVIES

Stephen King

1- I think that we're all mentally ill; those of us outside the asylums only hide it a little better—and maybe not all that much better, after all. We've all known people who talk to themselves, people who sometimes squinch their faces into horrible grimaces when they believe no one is

Source: *The Brief Prose Reader* Prentice Hall, 2003.

watching, people who have hysterical fears—of snakes, the dark, the tight place, the long drop . . . and, of course, those final worms and grubs that are waiting so patiently underground.

2- When we pay our four or five bucks and seat ourselves at tenth-row center in a theater showing a horror movie, we are daring the nightmare.

3- Why? Some of the reasons are simple and obvious. To show that we can, that we are not afraid, that we can ride this roller coaster. Which is not to say that a really good horror movie may not surprise a scream out of us at some point, the way we may scream when the roller coaster twists through a complete 360 or plows through a lake at the bottom of the drop. And horror movies, like roller coasters, have always been the special province of the young; by the time one turns 40 or 50, one's appetite for double twists or 360-degree loops may be considerably depleted.

4- We also go to re-establish our feelings of essential normality; the horror movie is innately conservative, even reactionary. Freda Jackson as the horrible melting woman in *Die, Monster, Die!* confirms for us that no matter how far we may be removed from the beauty of a Robert Redford or a Diana Ross, we are still light-years from true ugliness.

5- And we go to have fun.

6- Ah, but this is where the ground starts to slope away, isn't it? Because this is a very peculiar sort of fun, indeed. The fun comes from seeing others menaced—sometimes killed. One critic has suggested that if pro football has become the voyeur's version of combat, then the horror film has become the modern version of the public lynching.

7- It is true that the mythic, "fairy tale" horror film intends to take away the shades of gray . . . it urges us to put away our more civilized and adult penchant for analysis and to become children again, seeing things in pure blacks and whites. It may be that horror movies provide psychic relief on this level because this invitation to lapse into simplicity, irrationality, and even outright madness is extended so rarely. We are told we may allow our emotions a free rein . . . or no rein at all.

8- If we are all insane, then sanity becomes a matter of degree. If your insanity leads you to carve up women like Jack the Ripper or the Cleveland Torso Murderer, we slap you away in the funny farm (but neither of those two amateur-night surgeons was ever caught, heh-heh-heh); if, on the other hand, your insanity leads you only to talk to yourself when you're under stress or to pick your nose on your morning bus, then you are left alone to go about your business . . . though it is doubtful that you will ever be invited to the best parties.

9- The potential lyncher is in almost all of us (excluding saints, past and present; but, then, most saints have been crazy in their own ways), and every now and then, it has to be let loose to scream and roll around in the grass. Our emotions and our fears form their own body, and we recognize that it demands its own exercise to maintain proper muscle tone. Certain of these emotional muscles are accepted—even exalted—in civilized society; they are, of course, the emotions that tend to maintain the status quo of civilization itself. Love, friendship, loyalty, kindness—these are all the emotions that we applaud, emotions that have been immortalized in the couplets of Hallmark cards and in the verses (I don't dare call it poetry) of Leonard Nimoy.

10- When we exhibit these emotions, society showers us with positive reinforcement; we learn this even before we get out of diapers. When, as children, we hug our rotten little puke of a sister and give her a kiss, all the aunts and uncles smile and twitter and cry, "Isn't he the sweetest little thing?" Such coveted treats as chocolate-covered graham crackers often follow. But if we deliberately slam the rotten little puke of a sister's fingers in the door, sanctions follow—angry remonstrance from parents, aunts, and uncles: instead of a chocolate-covered graham cracker, a spanking.

11- But anti-civilization emotions don't go away, and they demand periodic exercise. We have such "sick" jokes as "What's the difference between a truckload of bowling balls and a truckload of dead babies?" Such a joke may surprise a laugh or a grin out of us even as we recoil, a possibility that confirms the thesis: If we share a common humanity, we also share a common insanity. None of which is intended as a defense of either the sick joke or insanity, but merely as an explanation of why the best horror films, like the best fairy tales, manage to be reactionary, anarchistic, and revolutionary all at the same time.

12- The mythic horror movie, like the sick joke, has a dirty job to do. It deliberately appeals to all that is worst in us. It is morbidity unchained, our most base instincts let free, our nastiest fantasies realized . . . and it all happens, fittingly enough, in the dark. For those reasons, good liberals often shy away from horror films. For myself, I like to see the most aggressive of them—*Dawn of the Dead*, for instance—as lifting a trap door in the civilized forebrain and throwing a basket of raw meat to the hungry alligators swimming around in that subterranean river beneath.

13- Why bother? Because it keeps them from getting out. It keeps them down there and me up here. It was Lennon and McCartney who said that all you need is love, and I would agree with that. As long as you keep the gators fed.

Fill in the chart below.

Cause	Effect
If we see the melting woman (4)	
When we see others menaced or sometimes killed (6)	
If we see horror movies (7)	
If you carve people up (8)	
If you pick your nose on the morning bus (8)	
If you show love, friendship and loyalty (10)	
If you show anti-civilized emotions (10)	
If you feed the alligators (your worst thoughts) (13)	

G. Definition

Preparing to Read

What would you say is the role of a wife? What is the role of a husband? As you read, notice the definitions Judy Brady gives to the word *wife*.

I WANT A WIFE

Judy Brady

1- I belong to that classification of people known as wives. I am A Wife. And, not altogether incidentally, I am a mother.

2- Not too long ago a male friend of mine appeared on the scene fresh from a recent divorce. He had one child, who is, of course, with his ex-wife. He is looking for another wife. As I thought about him while I was ironing one evening, it suddenly occurred to me that I, too, would like to have a wife. Why do I want a wife?

Source: *Strategies for College Writing* Prentice Hall, 2003.

3- I would like to go back to school so that I can become economically independent, support myself, and, if need be, support those dependent upon me. I want a wife who will work and send me to school. And while I am going to school, I want a wife to take care of my children. I want a wife to keep track of the children's doctor and dentist appointments. And to keep track of mine, too. I want a wife to make sure my children eat properly and are kept clean. I want a wife who will wash the children's clothes and keep them mended. I want a wife who is a good nurturing attendant to my children, who arranges for their schooling, makes sure that they have an adequate social life with their peers, takes them to the park, the zoo, etc. I want a wife who takes care of the children when they are sick, a wife who arranges to be around when the children need special care, because, of course, I cannot miss classes at school. My wife must arrange to lose time at work and not lose the job. It may mean a small cut in my wife's income from time to time, but I guess I can tolerate that. Needless to say, my wife will arrange and pay for the care of the children while my wife is working.

4- I want a wife who will take care of my physical needs. I want a wife who will keep my house clean. A wife who will pick up after my children, a wife who will pick up after me. I want a wife who will keep my clothes clean, ironed, mended, replaced when need be, and who will see to it that my personal things are kept in their proper place so that I can find what I need the minute I need it. I want a wife who cooks the meals, a wife who is a good cook. I want a wife who will plan the menus, do the necessary grocery shopping, prepare the meals, serve them pleasantly, and then do the cleaning up while I do my studying. I want a wife who will care for me when I am sick and sympathize with my pain and loss of time from school. I want a wife to go along when our family takes a vacation so that someone can continue to care for me and my children when I need a rest and change of scene.

5- I want a wife who will not bother me with rambling complaints about a wife's duties. But I want a wife who will listen to me when I feel the need to explain a rather difficult point I have come across in my course studies. And I want a wife who will type my papers for me when I have written them.

6- I want a wife who will take care of the details of my social life. When my wife and I are invited out by my friends, I want a wife who will take care of the baby-sitting arrangements. When I meet people at school that I like and want to entertain, I want a wife who will have the house clean, will prepare a special meal, serve it to me and my friends, and not interrupt when I talk about things that interest me and my friends. I want a wife who will have arranged that the children are fed and ready for bed before my guests arrive so that the children do not bother us. I want a wife who takes care of the needs of my guests so that they feel comfortable, who makes sure that they have an ashtray, that they are passed the hors d'oeuvres, that they are offered a second helping of the food, that their wine glasses are replenished when necessary, that their coffee is served to them as they like it. And I want a wife who knows that sometimes I need a night out by myself.

7- I want a wife who is sensitive to my sexual needs, a wife who makes love passionately and eagerly when I feel like it, a wife who makes sure that I am satisfied. And, of course, I want a wife who will not demand sexual attention when I am not in the mood for it. I want a wife who assumes the complete responsibility for birth control, because I do not want more children. I want a wife who will remain sexually faithful to me so that I do not have to clutter up my intellectual life with jealousies. And I want a wife who understands that my sexual needs may entail more than strict adherence to monogamy. I must, after all, be able to relate to people as fully as possible.

8- If, by chance, I find another person more suitable as a wife than the wife I already have, I want the liberty to replace my present wife with another one. Naturally, I will expect a fresh, new life; my wife will take the children and be solely responsible for them so that I am left free.

9- When I am through with school and have a job, I want my wife to quit working and remain at home so that my wife can more fully and completely take care of a wife's duties.

10- My God, who wouldn't want a wife?

Questions

1. According to the author, what are the characteristics of a wife?

   _____

   _____

   _____

   _____

   _____

   _____

_____

_____

_____

_____

_____

_____

_____

2. What transition words did you notice?

_____

CHAPTER SUMMARY

- **PATTERNS OF ORGANIZATION:** A pattern refers to how the sentences or ideas in a reading are structured or arranged. Recognizing the different patterns leads to improved comprehension.

- **TRANSITION WORDS:** Provide a bridge from one idea to another.

- **NARRATION:** A story or event usually told in first person. Tells who, what, why, when, and where. The sequence of events is important.

- **DESCRIPTION:** Uses details that appeal to the five senses. Creates visualization for the reader.

- **PROCESS ANALYSIS:** Shows with words a method of doing something. The sequence is extremely important. Look for steps and order.

- **CLASSIFICATION:** Divides a subject into various categories. Identifies a member or group based on similar characteristics. Look for part-to-whole relationships or various categories into which a large number of items can be sorted.

- **COMPARISON/CONTRAST:** Shows how two things are alike and/or different. The two things may be compared and contrasted subject by subject, or be compared and contrasted point by point.

- **CAUSE AND EFFECT:** Causes are reasons behind an event. Effects are results of events. This pattern often explains how or why the end result occurred.

- **DEFINITION:** Defines a person, place, thing or idea by explaining the characteristics that distinguish it from others in its class.

QUICK CONNECTIONS—CHAPTER SIX

News Source Connection

Narration: Using a newspaper or news magazine, locate a narrative selection. Make sure to remember that in news reporting the patterns are often intermixed, and a narrative is a retelling of an event. Clip the article from the newspaper or news magazine (print, if an online article) and highlight the example.

Description: Using a newspaper or news magazine, locate an article or part of an article that is describing an event, person, or place. With description, you are reading to find words that are intended to give a mental image of something experienced. Clip the article from the newspaper or news magazine (print, if an online article) and highlight the example.

Process: Using a newspaper or news magazine, locate an article describing a process. As you read, you are looking for gradual steps or changes that lead to a final result. Clip the article from the newspaper or news magazine (print, if an online article) and highlight the example.

Classification: Using a newspaper or news magazine, locate an article which includes an example of classification. You are reading to find information that has been divided into categories. Clip the article from the newspaper or news magazine (print, if an online article) and highlight the example.

Cause and effect: Using a newspaper or news magazine, locate a cause and effect article. Causal chains begin with a first cause, and follow with a series of events to reach a final conclusion or effect. Clip the article from the newspaper or news magazine (print, if an online article) and highlight the example.

Definition: Using a newspaper or news magazine, locate an article that defines a person, place, thing, or idea. You are reading to find information that identifies someone or something by distinct, clear, and detailed essential qualities. Clip the article from the newspaper or news magazine (print, if an online article) and highlight the example.

Textbook Connection

Narration: Using one of your own textbooks, locate a narrative selection. A narrative is retelling of an event. Mark the section within the text. Show your teacher to confirm.

Description: Using one of your own textbooks, locate a passage describing an event, person, or place. With description, you are reading to find words that are intended to give a mental image of something experienced. Mark the section within the text. Show your teacher to confirm.

Process: Using one of your own textbooks, locate a passage describing a process. As you read, you are looking for gradual steps or changes that lead to a final result. Mark the section within the text. Show your teacher to confirm.

Classification: Using one of your own textbooks, locate a passage which includes an example of classification. You are reading to find information that has been divided into categories. Mark the section within the text. Show your teacher to confirm.

Cause and effect: Using one of your own textbooks, locate a passage that includes a cause and effect relationship. Causal chains begin with a first cause, and follow with a series of events to reach a final conclusion or effect. Mark the section within the text. Show your teacher to confirm.

Definition: Using one of your own textbooks, locate a passage that defines a person, place, thing, or idea. You are reading to find information that identifies someone or something by distinct, clear, and detailed essential qualities. Mark the section within the text. Show your teacher to confirm.

Novel Connection

Narration: Choose a particular event, told in narrative style, that happened within a novel. Retell the event to the class, or you may choose to write it.

Description: Using a novel, choose a character to describe. This may be done as a verbal or written exercise.

Process: Using a problem from a novel, identify steps a character could use to solve the problem.

Classification: Using a novel, create a category chart for the characters, events, problems, emotions, heroes, villains, etc.

Cause and effect: List at least three of the various cause and effect experiences of two main characters within a novel.

Definition: Choose an idea or topic from a novel. Create a list of characteristics the author uses to define it.

Computer Connection

Using an online magazine or newspaper, read to locate examples of each of the six patterns described in this chapter.

Graphic Organizer Strategies

Chapter Preview

Graphic Organizer Strategies Overview

A. KWL

B. Concept Web (or the Five Ws)

C. Cause and Effect Chain

A graphic organizer is worth a thousand words . . .

Objectives

- Student will be able to organize pertinent information in a reading.
- Student will be able to extract main ideas from a reading.
- Student will use graphic organizer strategies to enhance comprehension.

Readiness Quiz

1. Read the article below. After reading, fill out the informational organizer.
2. As a class, go over the organizer. Discuss how to extract pertinent information.

ASIAN LADY BEETLES CAN BE SERIOUS HOUSEHOLD PESTS

Dennis Ferraro

Several of the common species of lady beetles, or ladybugs, will wander indoors during the fall. However, this is a distinctive and annoying trait of the Asian lady beetle, a relatively new species imported to the United States from eastern Asia.

The multicolored Asian lady beetle has become common in many areas of the eastern United States and Nebraska. This ladybug is beneficial and used as a natural control. It can also be a serious household pest in areas where it is well established.

Asian lady beetles, like boxelder bugs, pine seed bugs and elm leaf bugs, are accidental invaders. They wander indoors during a limited part of their life cycle, but they do not feed or reproduce indoors. They cannot attack the house structure, furniture or fabric. They cannot sting or carry disease. Lady beetles do not feed on people, but they might pinch exposed skin. Lady beetles may leave a slimy smear and they have a distinct odor when squashed.

As with other accidental invaders, the best management is to seal cracks, gaps and openings on the outside before the beetles wander in. A synthetic pyrethroid insecticide, such as permethrin, can be applied to the outside of the building. But to be effective, treatment must be applied before the beetles begin to enter buildings. Other home-use insecticides are ineffective.

What happened? _____

Who was there? _____

Why did it happen? _____

When did it happen? _____

Where did it happen? _____

Graphic Organizer Strategies Overview

Graphic organizers are visual images which can be used to represent information. There are various ways information can be organized, depending upon the material being read. A graphic organizer works well to simplify and organize material in one or more of the following ways:

- According to topics, main ideas and details
- In sequential order
- To show relationships between or among different things
- To show similarities and differences between two or more ideas or things
- By story elements
- . . . And many others!

Graphic organizers come in numerous forms. We will present three of the most widely used examples in this text, but there are many more examples on the Internet if you search for *graphic organizers*.

How Do They Work?

Graphic organizers provide visual representations of ideas, facts, theories, and concepts. They consist of circles, boxes, and other shapes, along with lines, to show connections. Creating a graphic organizer not only assists you in preparing and studying for a test; it can also provide you with a memorable visual *during* the test. Two features of an effective graphic organizer are **elaboration** and **personalization.** *Elaboration* is the use of colors, designs, and pictures to aid in memory. *Personalization* involves creating associations to the information on your graphic organizer with personal pictures or designs that make sense to you. These images will help you remember what is important. Following are descriptions of three common graphic organizers.

1. KWL

K: What do you already **know** about the topic? Brainstorm a list of such facts or ideas. This list represents your background or prior knowledge. The new information you learn, combined with your background knowledge, will create a new "file" of knowledge (old + new information).

W: What do you **want to learn?** Create a list of questions you'd like to answer from the new material. Use these questions as a focus for your reading. Then read to answer your questions.

L: What did you **learn?** Create a list of new information you learned from the reading.

Topic: Sharks

What I Know	What I Want to Know	What I Learned
Live in saltwater	How do they help humans?	Never get cancer
Swim all the time or die	What does their skin feel like?	Skin is like sand paper

2. Concept Web (or the Five Ws)

A concept web consists of a circle with branches to show the who, what, why, when, and where of a story, article, or any type of reading.

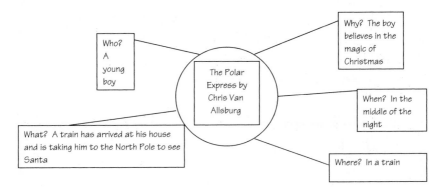

3. Cause and Effect Chain

Identifying cause and effect relationships enables the reader to focus on two important elements of comprehension: *what* happened and *why* it happened. Answering these questions helps the reader determine the consequences or results of specific behaviors or events. A cause is an action or event that makes something else (the effect) happen. A cause and effect chain shows the relationships between causes and effects, making them easier to see and understand.

To Practice
Use the following readings and graphic organizers for practice.

- KWL: Obsessive-Compulsive Disorder
- Concept Web: He's My Son!
- Cause and Effect Chain: The Open Window

QUICK TIP:

Remember information by using **elaboration** (designs, colors, patterns) and **personalization** (association to something familiar, pictures).

QUICK TIP:

When material seems disorganized or poorly organized, pay more attention to the headings, and read the summary first (if one is provided).

QUICK TIP:

Font size is generally an important clue to organizing information. A main heading in large font often indicates a main point. Each subheading in smaller font is an important point supporting the main point. When the font reverts to large again, you have a new idea, or the next main point.

FOR EXTRA PRACTICE

Use the readings in the Patterns of Organization chapter (see Chapter Six) of the text with the graphic organizers provided in this chapter.

A. KWL

Use the KWL chart that follows the article "Obsessive-Compulsive Disorder." Complete steps 1 and 2 before you read. After reading, complete step 4.

1. In the K column, list what you already know about the subject *Obsessive-Compulsive Disorder*.

2. In the *W* column, list what you want to learn (or questions you expect the reading to answer.)
3. Read "Obsessive-Compulsive Disorder," by Mary Lynn Hendrix.
4. After reading, in the *L* column, write down what you learned.

OBSESSIVE-COMPULSIVE DISORDER

Mary Lynn Hendrix

What is OCD?

In the mental illness called OCD, a person becomes trapped in a pattern of repetitive thoughts and behaviors that are senseless and distressing but extremely difficult to overcome. The following are typical examples of OCD:

> Troubled by the repeated thoughts that she may have contaminated herself by touching doorknobs and other "dirty" objects, a teenage girl spends hours every day washing her hands. Her hands are red and raw, and she has little time for social activities.

> A middle-aged man is tormented by the notion that he may injure others through carelessness. He has difficulty leaving his home because he must first go through a lengthy ritual of checking and rechecking the gas jets and water faucets to make certain that they are turned off.

If OCD becomes severe enough, it can destroy a person's capacity to function in the home, at work, or at school. That is why it is important to learn about the disorder and the treatments that are now available.

How Common is OCD?

For many years, mental health professionals thought of OCD as a very rare disease because only a small minority of their patients had the condition. But it is believed that many of those afflicted with OCD, in efforts to keep their repetitive thoughts and behaviors secret, fail to seek treatment. This has lead to underestimates of the number of people with the illness. However, a recent survey by the National Institute of Mental Health—the Federal agency that supports research nationwide on the brain, mental illness, and mental health—has provided new understanding about the prevalence of OCD. The NIMH survey shows that this disorder may affect as much as 2 percent of the population, meaning that OCD is more common than schizophrenia and other severe mental illnesses.

Source: *Building Strategies for College Reading,* Prentice Hall, 2001.

K-W-L Chart

What I Know	What I Want to Know	What I Learned

B. Concept Web (or the Five Ws)

1. Read "He's My Son!" by John Macionis.
2. After reading, use the concept web following the passage to fill in the who, what, why, when, and where of the short story.
3. Can you figure out the answer to the riddle at the end of the reading?

HE'S MY SON!

John Macionis

The automobile roared down the mountain road, tearing through sheets of windblown rain. Two people, a man and his young son, peered intently through the windshield, observing the edge of the road beyond which they could see only a black void. Suddenly, as the car rounded a bend, the headlights shone upon a large tree that had fallen across the roadway. The man swerved to the right and braked, but unable to stop, the car left the road, crashed through some brush, turned end upon end, and came to rest on its roof. Then a bit of good fortune: The noise of the crash had been heard at a nearby hunting lodge, and a telephone call from there soon brought police and a rescue crew. The driver, beyond help, was pronounced dead at the scene of the accident. Yet, the boy was still alive, although badly hurt and unconscious. Rushed by ambulance to the hospital in the town at the foot of the mountain, he was taken immediately into emergency surgery.

Alerted in advance, the medical team burst through the swinging doors ready to try to save the boy's life. Then, with a single look at his face, the surgeon abruptly exclaimed: "Oh, no! Get someone else to take over for me—I can't operate on this boy. *He's my son!*"

Answer to riddle (how can the boy be the surgeon's son?) _____

C. Cause and Effect Chain

1. Read "The Open Window," by Saki.
2. After reading, use the Cause and Effect Chain graphic organizer that follows the story to create a chain that depicts what happened and why.

Concept Web

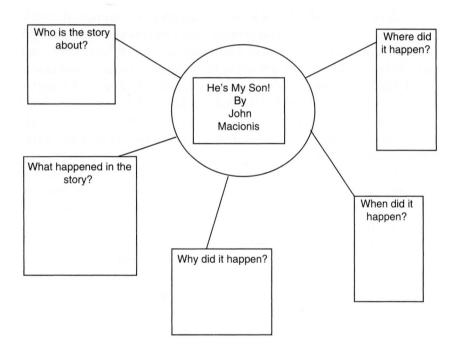

Who is the story about?

Where did it happen?

He's My Son!
By
John
Macionis

What happened in the story?

When did it happen?

Why did it happen?

THE OPEN WINDOW

Saki (H. H. Munro)

"My aunt will be down presently, Mr. Nuttel," said a very self-possessed young lady of fifteen; "in the meantime you must try and put up with me."

Framton Nuttel endeavored to say the correct something which should duly flatter the niece of the moment without unduly discounting the aunt that was to come. Privately he doubted more than ever whether these formal visits on a succession of total strangers would do much towards helping the nerve cure which he was supposed to be undergoing

"I know how it will be," his sister had said when he was preparing to migrate to this rural retreat; "you will bury yourself down there and not speak to a living soul, and your nerves will be worse than ever from moping. I shall just give you letters of introduction to all the people I know there. Some of them, as far as I can remember, were quite nice."

Framton wondered whether Mrs. Sappleton, the lady to whom he was presenting one of the letters of introduction, came into the nice division.

"Do you know many of the people round here?" asked the niece, when she judged that they had had sufficient silent communion.

"Hardly a soul," said Framton. "My sister was staying here, at the rectory, you know, some four years ago, and she gave me letters of introduction to some of the people here."

He made the last statement in a tone of distinct regret.

"Then you know practically nothing about my aunt?" pursued the self-possessed young lady.

"Only her name and address," admitted the caller. He was wondering whether Mrs. Sappleton was in the married or widowed state. An indefinable something about the room seemed to suggest masculine habitation.

"Her great tragedy happened just three years ago," said the child; "that would be since your sister's time."

"Her tragedy?" asked Framton; somehow in this restful country spot tragedies seemed out of place.

"You may wonder why we keep that window wide open on an October afternoon," said the niece, indicating a large French window that opened on to a lawn.

"It is quite warm for the time of the year," said Framton; "but has that window got anything to do with the tragedy?"

"Out through that window, three years ago to a day, her husband and her two young brothers went off for their day's shooting. They never came back. In crossing the moor to their favorite snipe-shooting ground they were all three engulfed in a treacherous piece of bog. It had been that dreadful wet summer, you know, and places that were safe in other years gave way suddenly without warning. Their bodies were never recovered. That was the dreadful part of it." Here the child's voice lost its self-possessed note and became falteringly human. "Poor aunt always thinks that they will come back someday, they and the little brown spaniel that was lost with them, and walk in at that window just as they used to do.

That is why the window is kept open every evening till it is quite dusk. Poor dear aunt, she has often told me how they went out, her husband with his white waterproof coat over his arm, and Ronnie, her youngest brother, singing 'Bertie, why do you bound?' as he always did to tease her, because she said it got on her nerves. Do you know, sometimes on still, quiet evenings like this, I almost get a creepy feeling that they will all walk in through that window—"

She broke off with a little shudder. It was a relief to Framton when the aunt bustled into the room with a whirl of apologies for being late in making her appearance.

"I hope Vera has been amusing you?" she said.

"She has been very interesting," said Framton.

"I hope you don't mind the open window," said Mrs. Sappleton briskly; "my husband and brothers will be home directly from shooting, and they always come in this way. They've been out for snipe in the marshes today, so they'll make a fine mess over my poor carpets. So like you men folk, isn't it?"

She rattled on cheerfully about the shooting and the scarcity of birds, and the prospects for duck in the winter. To Framton it was all purely horrible. He made a desperate but only partially successful effort to turn the talk on to a less ghastly topic, he was conscious that his hostess was giving him only a fragment of her attention, and her eyes were constantly straying past him to the open window and the lawn beyond. It was certainly an unfortunate coincidence that he should have paid his visit on this tragic anniversary.

"The doctors agree in ordering me complete rest, an absence of mental excitement, and avoidance of anything in the nature of violent physical exercise," announced Framton, who labored under the tolerably widespread delusion that total strangers and chance acquaintances are hungry for the least detail of one's ailments and infirmities, their cause and cure. "On the matter of diet they are not so much in agreement," he continued.

"No?" said Mrs. Sappleton, in a voice which only replaced a yawn at the last moment. Then she suddenly brightened into alert attention—but not to what Framton was saying.

"Here they are at last!" she cried. "Just in time for tea, and don't they look as if they were muddy up to the eyes!"

Framton shivered slightly and turned towards the niece with a look intended to convey sympathetic comprehension. The child was staring out through the open window with a dazed horror in her eyes. In a chill shock of nameless fear Framton swung round in his seat and looked in the same direction.

In the deepening twilight three figures were walking across the lawn towards the window; they all carried guns under their arms, and one of them was additionally burdened with a white coat hung over his shoulders. A tired brown spaniel kept close at their heels. Noiselessly they neared the house, and then a hoarse young voice chanted out of the dusk: "I said, Bertie, why do you bound?"

Framton grabbed wildly at his stick and hat; the hall door, the gravel drive, and the front gate were dimly noted stages in his headlong retreat. A cyclist coming along the road had to run into the hedge to avoid imminent collision.

"Here we are, my dear," said the bearer of the white mackintosh, coming in through the window, "fairly muddy, but most of it's dry. Who was that who bolted out as we came up?"

"A most extraordinary man, a Mr. Nuttel," said Mrs. Sappleton; "could only talk about his illnesses, and dashed off without a word of goodbye or apology when you arrived. One would think he had seen a ghost."

"I expect it was the spaniel," said the niece calmly; "he told me he had a horror of dogs. He was once hunted into a cemetery somewhere on the banks of the Ganges by a pack of pariah dogs, and had to spend the night in a newly dug grave with the creatures snarling and grinning and foaming just above him. Enough to make anyone lose their nerve."

Romance at short notice was her specialty.

Cause-and-Effect Chain

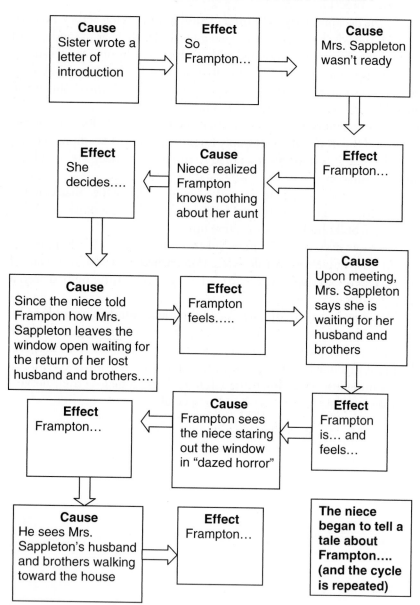

CHAPTER SUMMARY

- **GRAPHIC ORGANIZERS:** Graphic Organizers are used to create visual representations of ideas, facts, theories, and concepts.

- **ELABORATION:** Elaboration is the use of colors, designs, and pictures to aid in remembering information.

- **PERSONALIZATION:** Personalization is creating associations to the information on your graphic organizer with personal pictures or designs that makes sense to you.

- **KWL:** A graphic organizer that helps to identify a reader's prior knowledge and to connect it with new information.

- **CONCEPT WEB:** A graphic organizer that helps to identify who the reading is about, what happened, why it happened, when it happened, and where it happened.

- **CAUSE AND EFFECT CHAIN:** A graphic organizer that helps to identify cause and effect relationships in a reading. Focuses on two important elements: what happened, and why.

QUICK CONNECTIONS—CHAPTER SEVEN

News Source Connection

Using the concept web format located within the chapter, choose a newspaper or news magazine article. Read the article and fill out a concept web.

Textbook Connection

Choose one of your own textbooks. Use the KWL chart format located within the chapter. Before you read, write down what you know about the topic in the **K** column. Before you read, write down what you want to know in the **W** column. Read. After reading, record the answers to your questions and/or new things you learned about the topic in the **L** column.

Novel Connection

Using a novel, select a problem the characters are experiencing within the novel. Create a cause and effect chain as shown in this chapter.

Computer Connection

Go to a news source web site such as *Time* or the *New York Times* web site. Find an article and create your own graphic organizer. Personalize it! Add color! Feel free to place information in ways that give meaning to you.

Computer Reading and Writing

Chapter Preview

Computer Reading and Writing Strategies Overview

A. How to Search the Internet
   1. The World Wide Web
   2. Four Key Factors
   3. How to Begin

B. Evaluating Websites
   1. Does the site meet the purpose of your search?
   2. Is the site easy to use? (design and navigability)
   3. How valid is the information found?

C. Word Processing Basics—A Reference Guide

Ability to use a computer to read and write in college . . . Priceless

Strategy Area A: How to Search the Internet

Objective

- Student will be able to conduct an Internet search for specific information using the following basics:

  1. Definition of World Wide Web

  2. Four key factors involved in each search

  3. How to begin a search

Readiness Quiz A

Choose **T** for true and **F** for false after reading each statement below.

1. _____ A browser is a page that contains information, pictures, and video clips about a specific topic.

2. _____ A search engine is a computerized index to find information on the WWW.

3. _____ W3 is a math symbol, not a computer term.

4. _____ Opening a link from a web page takes concentration and memory.

5. _____ Plus signs can help you narrow your search.

6. _____ Boolean searching involves the use of the words AND, OR, AND-NOT.

7. _____ To search, just type a question into a search box.

Note: If you are a beginner in the area of computer basics (especially word processing), you may want to check out the readiness quiz and accompanying reference guide in Part C of this chapter before starting Parts A and B of the chapter.

Computer Reading and Writing Strategies Overview

In today's world, we acquire information in a broadening variety of ways. PDAs, Ipods, the Internet, and text messaging are a few of the innovations that have changed the ways in which we gather data. To adapt to our ever-growing technical/digital environment, we need to broaden our reading strategies too. Part A of this chapter will help you learn how to search the Internet, and Part B will help you determine which sites contain reliable information. Once you know how to do both, you'll be able to use the Internet to find valid information on just about any topic. Part C covers some word processing basics and is a reference guide for those who might need that kind of assistance, as well.

A. How to Search the Internet

The first strategy involved in reading on the Internet is searching to find the information you want to read. Whether for academics or pleasure, to find relevant information *quickly* you need to know how to search the Internet. The first section of this chapter will show you how to conduct an efficient Internet search.

1. The World Wide Web

The World Wide Web (WWW, or W3) is an interconnected, hypertext-based network that allows you to browse a variety of Internet resources organized by home pages. The WWW is incredibly vast. This is positive because there is so much information available, but it can be negative because anyone with a little computer knowledge can create a web page. When you do a search, you must realize that there is an extensive amount of unreliable, as well as reliable, information.

2. Four Key Factors

Browser: A browser is a program that provides a way of looking at the information on the WWW.

The two major browsers are Microsoft's Internet Explorer and Netscape's Navigator.

Search Engine: A computerized index to information on the WWW.

Four Popular Search Engines
www.ask.com
www.google.com
www.msn.com
www.yahoo.com

Web page: A document location or site that provides information on your search topic(s). It may contain pictures, video clips, audio clips, charts, graphs, links, and more.

QUICK TIP:

Remember, anyone can make a web page. When you search, use the strategies in Part B to make sure you find valid information.

Link: An automatic "address jump" to another site containing similar or more information on your search topic. Just click on a link, and you're at a new website!

3. How to Begin

1. Formulate a question on a topic you'd like to research.
2. Choose the important words from the question or topic sentence.

   Question: What was the Revolutionary War and who was involved?
   Important words: Revolutionary War

3. Type the important words into your search box located on your search engine home page.

4. Look at your results. Choose and open the web page you think will best help you answer your question.

QUICK TIP:

You may open and close several web pages from your results until you find the one with the reliable information you are seeking.

Tips for Narrowing Your Search

Quotation Marks	Used around words that must appear together, in a specific order within your search	"Social Justice"
Plus Signs	Used before words that must both appear in your results	+ "Social Justice" + environment
Minus Signs	Used before terms you do not want to appear in the results	+ "Social Justice" + environment − animals
Boolean Searching	Use AND, OR, AND-NOT	"Social Justice" AND environment NOT animals

Another important aspect of conducting a useful search is knowing how to use the Toolbar. Since most computers use Microsoft programs, we've included the following information about the Explorer Toolbar.

UNDERSTANDING THE EXPLORER TOOLBAR

The Explorer Bar includes functions relevant only to the browser itself.

- The Back and Forward arrows allow you to move back and forth between websites previously visited.

- When you click the Back key on the Toolbar, you go to the last page you visited. The browser stores several pages, so you can click the key until the one you want becomes available to you.

- Click the Forward key to reverse the list order.

- When you click the Back key down arrow, you may select the specific page you want to see from the drop-down list.

- The Stop button lets you terminate a command if you decide that it is taking too long.

- The Refresh button updates the current page to include changes that might have taken place since you accessed the site.

- Home sends you back to your designated Home Page.

- Search opens up search options.

- Favorites opens up your list of favorite sites in a separate window on the left side of your screen.

- History opens a list of previously visited sites.

- When you click the History button on the Toolbar, you may select the page you want to see. If the calendar entries are compressed, click the calendar icon to see the list of sites you visited during the week or during the day.

- Mail opens your mailbox options.

- Print allows you to print a current web page.

Now you should be ready to try a search! Search the Internet to find answers to the questions that follow. Fill in the important words that you'll need to type into the search box, do the search, and then fill in the answer to each question.

1. Question: What is the difference between an isosceles triangle and a right triangle?

   Important words: _____

   Search It!

   Answer from results: _____

2. Question: Who wrote the classic novel *To Kill a Mockingbird?*

   Important words: _____

   Search it!

   Answer from results: _____

3. Question: Define, describe, and draw the three major rock types in earth science.

   Important words: _____

   Search it!

   Answer from results:

Rock Type	Definition	Drawing
1.		
2.		
3.		

4. Question: Compare and contrast AIDS and gonorrhea.

   Important words: _____

   Search it!

   Answer from results:

AIDS and Gonorrhea

Similarities	Differences

Strategy Area B: Evaluating Websites

Objective:

- Student will be able to evaluate Internet websites for their usefulness, based on three criteria:

  1. Does the site meet the purpose of your search?

  2. Is the site easy to use? (design and navigability)

  3. How valid is the information found?

Readiness Quiz B

Choose **T** for true or **F** for false after reading each statement below.

1. _____ Information found on the Internet is current.

2. _____ It is primarily the instructor's responsibility to check the reliability and validity of information used in students' course assignments.

3. _____ The government regulates all Internet websites so we know they're factual.

4. _____ Anyone can create a website and have it on the Internet.

5. _____ You can tell certain things about a website from its address.

6. _____ It's difficult to tell if a website is someone's personal page.

7. _____ The first step to finding information on the Internet is to use a search engine.

1. Does the Site Meet the Purpose of Your Search?

Don't just start your search by going to Google or Yahoo! and typing in a couple of words!

You need to start by asking yourself, "What is the purpose of this search?" or "What is my research goal?" Once you've determined a research goal, you can screen sites by comparing them with your research goal. To determine your research goal, ask yourself questions like these: Do I want facts, opinions, reasoned arguments, statistics, narratives, eyewitness reports, or descriptions? Is the purpose of my search to find new ideas, or is it to find either factual or reasoned support for a position? Do I want to survey opinion? Do I want graphics, photos or illustrations? Determine exactly what kind of information you need for your assignment. If you're not sure, check with your instructor before you determine your research goal.

QUICK TIP:

Always set a research goal before you start your information search!

Once you've set your research goal, you can begin your search using the strategies in Part A of this chapter. As you open up sites that you're considering for your research, skim over each one to see if it seems to meet your research goal. If it appears to have the information you're looking for according to your goal, then you're ready to apply the next two strategies to see if the site is one you want to use.

2. Is the Site Easy to Use? (Design and Navigability)

There are several factors which should indicate rapidly how easy a site will be for you to use. The two major ones are the site's *design*, or set-up and appearance, and its *navigability*, or how easy it is to get around in the site.

A site's design includes factors such as colors, background, size and font of print, and graphics. Are these things pleasing to the eye and easy to see? Or are they jumbled and distracting? Is there a clear order for finding information, or does it seem confusing?

Navigability of a site means the ability to get around in, or use, the site. The design of the site contributes to its navigability. Are the different sections of the site clearly marked and easy to find? Is there always a link back to the home page? Are links to other sites easily identified? Are the links "hot," meaning can you click right on them and be taken to the linked site? Are the links up to date?

QUICK TIP:

Quickly skim over the home page of a site to get a feel for it. Is it pleasing to your eye? Does it make sense to you? Does it seem easy to start finding information?

If your impressions of the site are favorable so far, continue on to the third strategy for evaluating the site: Is the information found on the site valid and acceptable for use with your assignment?

3. How Valid is the Information Found?

Determining the validity of the information on a website is the most important part of the evaluation process. If the information is not reliable and valid, it doesn't matter if it fits your research goal or is easy to use; the site is worthless to you! Often the most important part of a process tends to be the most time-consuming, but it doesn't have to be. Below are some quick ways to check the validity of a site. Start by finding the answers to these questions:

1. **Sponsor:** What kind of organization sponsors the site? The answer can be found by looking at the last three letters in the address, or URL (Uniform Resource Locator). Addresses which end with the letters **edu** (education), **gov** (government), **mil** (military) or **org** (nonprofit organization) are usually reputable sites. Addresses ending in **com** or **net** are commercial addresses, which means they're generally trying to make money in some way. Information on these sites can be reliable, but you need to do more checking

than you would on the nonprofit sites. Sites which are personal web pages set up by individuals are the least likely to be reliable. A site that ends with ~*name* (a personal name), % *name*, or a name followed by the words *people, users,* or *members,* indicates a personal website—which means, be careful!! These sites, while not necessarily unreliable, require more investigation from the reader because the information is not backed by a domain owner or publisher.

QUICK TIP:

The last three letters of the URL are the quickest way to judge validity of a website.

2. **Author:** Who's responsible for the information? The top or bottom of the web page should identify the person responsible for putting it up and maintaining it (the webmaster of the site). Look for the author's institutional affiliation or other credentials. Is there documentation of the author or a bibliography of his work?

   What are the author's credentials and reputation? If the author is an expert and is qualified to write about the information contained at the site, it should be clearly stated. Look for a link to background information about the author, or better yet, a curriculum vita. Make sure information is truly produced by this expert, and is not posted erroneously or fraudulently.

3. **Date:** How old is the information? Remember, wide use of the Internet has been around for more than ten years, so you can't automatically assume that information you find on the Net is current. Look for the date that the site was last revised, which is usually found at the bottom of the home page. Even if the date is fairly recent, remember that it doesn't mean that all of the information on the site was revised on that date. However, a recent update may mean that the site is well maintained, which is a good indicator of current information.

4. **Content:** Where did the information originate? What seems to be the purpose of the site? Again, the last three letters of the address tell you a lot about the source of the information and if the site is commercial or nonprofit. This is a good place to use your skimming skills. A quick skim of a few pages should help you begin to determine the comprehensiveness of the material, its accuracy, whether it contains more fact or opinion, if it's written from a scholarly point of view, if it seems to be promoting a particular viewpoint, or if it's advertising. Check to see if the information is documented in some way. Is there a bibliography or other list of sources? Has anyone reviewed the site? Keep in mind that there are specialized guides to help you. One example: *Guides to Internet Resources: The Best of the Net.*

5. **Copyright:** If information is reproduced from another source or publication, check for permission to reproduce and/or copyright details. The following two sites evaluate websites before including them:

http://www2.lib.udel.edu/subj/internet/index.htm

http://www.sau.edu/bestinfo/index.htm

[*Best Information on the Net (BIOTN)*]

Guide sites like these also list the resources by subject matter. Using specialized guide sites can save you time in two ways. First, you know the site is valid, so it doesn't require much checking on your part. Second, when you click on the topic or subject you're researching, you obtain rapid access to several reliable sites.

QUICK TIP:

Use a specialized guide to find valid sites quickly.

6. **Corroboration:** Did you corroborate your sources? Corroboration, or finding the information in more than one place, is an important test of truth. It's a good idea to triangulate your sources, that is, find at least three sources that agree. If the sources do not agree, do

further research to find out how wide the disagreement is before you draw your conclusions. If you can't find other sites with the same, or similar information, be wary of trusting the validity of information.

There are a couple of simple ways to evaluate websites. The first is to go to

http://www.lib.berkeley.edu/TeachingLib/Guides/Internet/ EvalWorksheet.pdf

to print off a checklist that helps you determine if a site is valid and useful for your purpose. Or you can use a simpler checklist (see below.) Once you've had enough practice finding and evaluating websites which fulfill your research goals, you won't need to use a checklist. You'll *automatically* find yourself checking the points mentioned to evaluate a site more rapidly. Won't that be great? The bottom line: Always evaluate any site you plan to use in your academic work, particularly the validity of the site. Don't skip this step to save time. You might be putting your college success in jeopardy.

QUICK TIP:

ALWAYS check the validity of a site before using it for academic purposes. Don't risk getting a low grade for using incorrect information.

See the next page for the *Quick* Website Evaluation Checklist. You can tear it out and make copies to use when you do Internet research.

QUICK TIP:

Filling out a checklist sheet for each source you use makes it quick and easy to cite your sources on the Reference page of your written document.

Quick Website Evaluation Checklist

Research goal:

Site name:

Site address:

1. Sponsor (last three letters of site address, tells where the site originates from):

2. Author (what person and/or organization is responsible for the content?):

3. Date of article or information:

4. Content:

5. Copyright:

6. Corroboration—find three other sites with the same information:

   a.

   b.

   c.

Site reviews:

Usability:

Strategy Area C: Word Processing Basics— A Reference Guide

Objective

- Student will be able to review some of the basic concepts of word processing using the reference guide in this section.

Readiness Quiz C

Choose **T** for true or **F** for false after reading each statement below.

1. _____ I know how to use a word processing standard toolbar.

2. _____ I know how to create a new document.

3. _____ I know how to edit a document.

4. _____ I know how to save a document.

5. _____ I know how to reopen a saved document.

6. _____ I know how to format a document.

If you answered **F** to any of the above statements, please refer to the appropriate section of the reference guide on the pages which follow.

C. Word Processing Basics—A Reference Guide

The purpose of this section is to give you a quick reference guide to creating documents. Most of the work you do in a college classroom will require completed computer documents (typed). Often, students have not received computer training, but have assumed skills by watching others. Some students have not had any computer experience in creating a document, but can surf the Net. Some students have no computer experience at all. This is a straightforward guide to working with Microsoft Word, a software program available on most computers in colleges across the country.

Basic Word Processing Reference Guide for Microsoft Word

THE STANDARD TOOLBAR

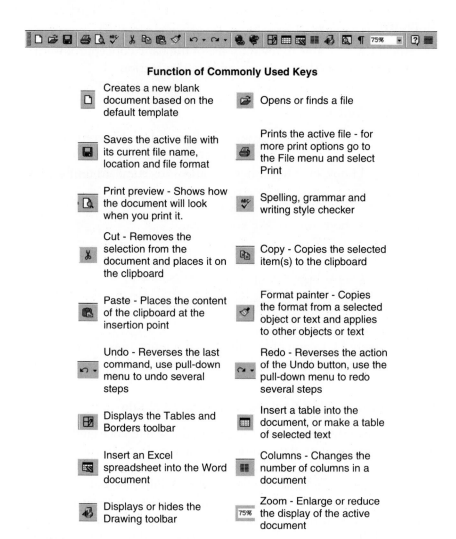

Function of Commonly Used Keys

Creates a new blank document based on the default template

Opens or finds a file

Saves the active file with its current file name, location and file format

Prints the active file - for more print options go to the File menu and select Print

Print preview - Shows how the document will look when you print it.

Spelling, grammar and writing style checker

Cut - Removes the selection from the document and places it on the clipboard

Copy - Copies the selected item(s) to the clipboard

Paste - Places the content of the clipboard at the insertion point

Format painter - Copies the format from a selected object or text and applies to other objects or text

Undo - Reverses the last command, use pull-down menu to undo several steps

Redo - Reverses the action of the Undo button, use the pull-down menu to redo several steps

Displays the Tables and Borders toolbar

Insert a table into the document, or make a table of selected text

Insert an Excel spreadsheet into the Word document

Columns - Changes the number of columns in a document

Displays or hides the Drawing toolbar

Zoom - Enlarge or reduce the display of the active document

Creating a Document

1. Open Microsoft Word by clicking on the icon or locating it by pressing the Start key.

2. Begin to type your document.

   • Press the Enter key only to start a new paragraph.

- Use the Backspace key or the Delete key to remove unwanted letters, words, or sentences.

3. As you type, save what you have done every 10 to 15 minutes.
4. If a word is underlined with a red or green wavy line, right-click on the word, and select from the list of suggested spellings or grammar corrections.
5. Use the Print Preview ⬚ key to see what your document will look like once you have printed it.
6. If it looks the way you would like for it to look, save it before printing.
7. To print, click the Print ⬚ key on the standard tool bar.
8. To close your document, click the File menu, and select the Close option, or click the X in top right corner of page.

Editing a Document

1. Highlight the text to be moved or copied.
2. Click the Cut ⬚ key if you want to move the text to a different location *or*
3. Click the Copy ⬚ key if you want to copy the text.
4. Click where you want to paste the text, and then click the Paste ⬚ key.

Saving a Document

1. Click the Save ⬚ button on the standard tool bar.
2. Select Local Disk (C:) to save on the hard drive.
3. To save to a floppy disk or flash drive:
   - Click the Save ⬚ button.
   - Click the down arrow in the list box.
   - Click A drive to save to the floppy; click F drive to save to the flash drive.
   - Type the file name in the File Name list box.
   - Click Save at the lower right corner of the dialog box.

Reopening a Document

1. Open Microsoft Word.
2. Click the Open 📂 key on the standard tool bar.
3. Click the drop-down arrow to specify the drive [Local Disk (C) or $3^1/_2$ Floppy A or Flash Drive (F)].
4. Double-click the file name from the list of files available.

Formatting a Document

THE FORMATTING TOOLBAR

| Normal ▾ | Arial ▾ | 12 ▾ | **B** | *I* | U | ≣ ≣ ≣ ≣ | ⅛≣ ☷ ≣ ≣ | ☐ ▾ ✐ ▾ A ▾ |

	Function of Commonly Used Buttons		
Normal ▾	Select the style to apply to paragraphs	Arial ▾	Changes the font of the selected text
12 ▾	Changes the size of selected text and numbers	**B**	Makes selected text and numbers bold
I	Makes selected text and numbers italic	U	Underlines selected text and numbers
≣	Aligns to the left with a ragged right margin	≣	Centers the selected text
≣	Aligns to the right with a ragged left margin	≣	Aligns the selected text to both the left and right margins
⅛≣	Makes a numbered list or reverts back to normal	☷	Add, or remove, bullets in a selected paragraph
≣	Decreases the indent to the previous tab stop	≣	Indents the selected paragraph to the next tab stop
☐ ▾	Adds or removes a border around selected text or objects	✐ ▾	Marks text so that it is highlighted and stands out
A ▾	Formats the selected text with the color you click		

Formatting a Document

1. Highlight the text to be formatted.

2. Change the style of the text by clicking the Bold **B** , Italic *I* , or Underline U key from the Formatting Toolbar.

3. Change the font type by selecting a font from the Font List Arial ▾ on the Formatting Toolbar.

4. Change the font size by selecting the size from the Font Size 12 ▾ list on the Formatting Toolbar.

5. Create a bulleted or numbered list by clicking the Bullets key or the Numbering key.

6. Create a border around the page by clicking the Format menu, borders and shading, page border, and then select the border you like.

7. Change the document's margins by clicking the File menu, page set-up, margin tab, and then adjust the margins.

8. Add a header or footer by clicking the View menu, header and footer, then type what will be shown in the area.

9. Double-space the document by clicking the Format menu, paragraph, line spacing, and then select Double from the drop-down list.

QUICK TIP:

Remember . . . You can undo most actions by using one of the following: clicking the Undo arrow, using Control Z, or going to the Edit menu, and selecting Undo Typing.

CHAPTER SUMMARY

- **SEARCHING THE INTERNET:** In order to search effectively on the Internet, it's important to be familiar with the term and concept of the World Wide Web, to understand four key factors involved in a search, and to know the basics of beginning a search.

- **WORLD WIDE WEB (WWW, OR W3):** An interconnected, hypertext-based network that allows you to browse a variety of Internet resources organized by home pages.

- **FOUR KEY FACTORS:** Include use of a browser, a search engine, web pages, and links.

- **BEGINNING A SEARCH:** Involves familiarity with the Explorer Toolbar, determining the topic of the search, identifying key words for the search, knowing where to type those key words, and finally, analyzing the search results and understanding how to narrow the search.

- **EVALUATING WEBSITES:** Entails determining the purpose of the search and then analyzing sites for ease of use and validity of information.

  - **Purpose of Search:** To save time and effort, set a research goal before beginning the search for information. Determine what type of site will best meet your goal.

  - **Ease of Use:** Major factors include a site's design and its navigability. Skim the home page (and other pages) for eye appeal and ease of use. Determine if it's organized in a sensible way.

  - **Validity of Information:** Determining the validity of the information on a website is the most important part of the evaluation process. Things to consider include the sponsor and author of the site, the dates of the information on the site and when it was last updated, the content itself, copyright issues, and whether or not other sites or sources corroborate the content of the site.

- **WORD PROCESSING BASICS:** Consult the brief guide at the end of this chapter for basic information on using a standard toolbar, and for creating, editing, saving, reopening, and formatting documents.

QUICK CONNECTIONS—CHAPTER EIGHT

News Source Connection

Using the Internet, find and skim three different news websites to compare and contrast the reports on a current event topic of your choice. Be sure to identify the websites used. You may report your results in paragraph format, or you may use a graphic organizer such as a comparison/contrast chart.

Textbook Connection

Use a textbook from one of your other classes (or a sample chapter provided by your instructor). Select an interesting topic which is addressed in the text or sample chapter. Then use the Internet to search for, and list, websites that address the same topic. Check for corroboration of specific ideas between the sites and the text. Write a brief report on your findings, and be sure to include your list of sites.

Novel Connection

Use the Internet to locate additional information on the author of a novel you are reading in your current reading class. Create a list of sites you found, and write a one-page summary of your findings.

Computer Connection

Choose a topic from this course (or one of your other courses this term) to research on the Internet. Find at least five sites, and list them. Evaluate two of the five sites, using either of the evaluation checklists included in this chapter or the following website:

http://www.quick.org.uk/menu.htm

Use a word processor to type a brief report on your findings.

Below are some other sites you could use instead of, or in addition to, the site listed above:

http://www.lib.berkeley.edu/TeachingLib/Guides/Internet/Evaluate.html

http://www.library.cornell.edu/olinuris/ref/research/webeval.html

http://www.library.cornell.edu/olinuris/ref/research/webcrit.html

http://www.virtualchase.com/quality/

http://www.multcolib.org/homework/webeval.html

Credits

Chapter 7

Chapter 8

Index

A

Albom, M., 93, 95
Analyzing, 75–85
  fact and opinion, 76–78
  identifying author attitude, bias,
    tone, assumptions, 82–85
  identifying writer's prupose, 75–76
  and synthesizing, definition of, 85
  validity, judging, 78–82
Appendix, 46
  definition of, 60
Arbetter, S., 120–24
Assumptions
  definition of, 86
  identifying, 82–85
Author, of website, 163
Author attitude
  definition of, 86
  identifying, 82–85

B

Bee, H., 71
Bias
  definition of, 86
  identifying, 82–85
Brady, J., 130–32
Bridging, of ideas, 112
Browser, 155

C

Cause and effect, 110, 111, 112,
  127–30
  chain, 141, 146, 150, 151
  definition of, 133

Childress, S., 71
Classification, 110, 111, 112,
  120–25
  definition of, 133
Closed syllables, 11
Clue words, 86
Comparison/contrast, 110, 111,
  112, 125–27
  definition of, 133
Comprehension strategies, 27–41
  comprehension, improving,
    38–40
  details, identifying, 35–38
  main ideas, identifying, 30–35
  SQ3R technique, 39, 40
  topics, identifying, 27–30
Computer reading and writing
  strategies, 155–74
  beginning search, 156–57
  browser, 155
  evaluating websites, 161–66
  Internet searches, 155–61
  link, 156
  search engine, 156
  web page, 156
  word processing basics, 167–71
Concept web, 141, 145
  definition of, 151
Conclusions, drawing in reading,
  69–73
  definition of, 85
  practice in, 72–73
Connotation, 21–22, 23
Content, website, 164

Context clues, 3–9
  contrast, 4, 6–7, 22
  definition, 4–5, 22
  example, 4, 5–6, 22
  inference, 4, 7–8, 22
  using in paragraphs, 8–9
Contrast. *See* Comparison/contrast
Contrast clues, 4, 6–7, 22
Contreras, J., 71
Copyright, of website, 164
Corroboration, on website, 164–65
Critical reading strategies
  analyzing and synthesizing, 75–85
  drawing conclusions, 69–73
  making inferences, 69–73
  predicting, 65–69
Critical thinking, 85
3C technique, 52–54
  definition of, 60

D

Date, website, 163
Definition, 110, 111, 112, 130–33
  clues, 4–5, 22
Denotation, 21–22, 23
Description, 110, 111, 115–17
  definition of, 133
Design, of websites, 161–62
Details, 75
  definition of, 40
  identifying, 35–38
  major, 37–38, 40
  minor, 37–38, 40
  SQ3R technique, using, 36–37
  5 W and H questions, using, 35
Dictionary
  connotation in, 21–22, 23
  definitions in, 21
  denotation in, 21–22, 23
  using, 69
DiLorenzo, 35
Doran, M., 68

E

Elaboration, 140, 142
  definition of, 151
Emerson, R.W., 101
Emotional appeal, 79
Erickson, 35
Essay, 34
Evaluate, 76, 85
Evidence, 78
  source of, 78
Example clues, 4, 5–6, 22

F

Fact, 76–78
  definition of, 85
Fallacy, 82
False cause, 81
Ferraro, D., 138
Figurative language, definition of,
  102
Figurative language strategies,
  91–105
  hyperbole, 100–102
  metaphor, 91–97
  personification, 98–99
  simile, 91–97
Five Ws. *See* Concept web
Flash cards, 22
Ford, J., 98–99

G

Gibran, K., 98
Glossary, 46
  definition of, 60
Goldberg, L., 125–27
Goldwater, B., 33
Google, 161
Graphic organizers, definition of, 151
Graphic organizer strategies,
  140–52
  cause and effect chain, 141
  concept web (five Ws), 141

KWL, 140–41, 142–43
  purpose of, 140
Greek prefixes, 15
  number/negative, 16
Greek roots, 10, 14, 17–19, 20, 39

H

Hawthorne, N., 76
Hazy generalization, 80
Hendrix, M.L., 143
Highlighting, 49, 51
  triple, 54–56
Hughes, L., 113–15
Hyperbole, 91, 100–102
  definition of, 103
  practice in, 101–2

I

Index, 46
  definition of, 60
Inference clues, 4, 7–8, 22
Inferences
  definition of, 85
  making in reading, 69–73
Internet, 155–61
  searches, 156–57, 171
  World Wide Web, 155
Internet Explorer (Microsoft), 155
  understanding toolbar in, 158
Interpret, 76, 85

J

Johnson, 34

K

Keillor, G., 117–20
King, S., 127–29
Kirkpatrick, B., 100
Kluger, Jeffrey, 59
KWL, 140–41, 142–43
  chart, 144
  definition of, 151

L

Latin prefixes, 15
  number/negative, 16
Latin roots, 10, 14, 17–19, 20, 39
Link, 156

M

Macionis, J., 145
Main ideas, 27, 37, 75, 110
  definition of, 40
  identifying, 30–35, 38
Major details, 37–38
  definition of, 40
  identifying, 38
Martel, Y., 67
McCarthy, T., 30
McGinn, D., 99
McNally, 34
Metaphor, 91–97
  definition of, 102–3
  practice in using, 93–97
Microsoft Word, 167–71
  creating document, 168–69
  editing document, 169
  formatting document, 170–71
  formatting toolbar, 170
  reopening document, 170
  saving document, 169
  standard toolbar for, 168
Minor details, 37–38
  definition of, 40
Mnemonics, 22
Munro, H.H., 146–49

N

Name-calling, 80
Narration, 110, 111, 113–15
  definition of, 133
Navigability, of websites, 161–62
Negative words, 83
Netscape Navigator, 155
Number/negative prefixes, 16

O

O'Hara, F., 96
Oliver, W.M., 29
Olsen, 29
Omaha World Herald, 76, 78
Open syllables, 11
Opinion, 76–78, 83
  all or nothing, 80
  definition of, 85
Organizational patterns
  aspects of, 111–12
  definition of, 133
  purpose of, 111

P

Paragraphs
  identifying details in, 36
  topics in, 28–30
Patterns of organization strategies,
    110–35
  cause and effect, 110, 111, 112,
    127–30
  classification, 110, 111, 112,
    120–25
  comparison/contrast, 110, 111,
    112, 125–27
  definition, 110, 111, 112, 130–33
  description, 110, 111, 115–17
  narration, 110, 111, 113–15
  process analysis, 110, 111,
    117–20
Pelzer, D., 70
Personalization, 140, 142
  definition of, 151
Personification, 91, 98–99
  definition of, 103
  practice in, 99
Poetry, figurative language use in,
    91
Positive words, 83
Predicting
  definition of, 85
  in reading, 65–69

Preface, 46
  definition of, 60
Prefix, 10, 12–14, 23
  Greek, 15
  Latin, 15
  number/negative, 16
Preview, 57
Process analysis, 110, 111, 117–20
  definition of, 133
Purpose, writer's
  definition of, 85
  identifying, 75–76

R

Reading
  3C technique, using, 52–54
  methods, for textbooks, 48–56
  preparation for, 117, 125, 127,
    130
  speed, 59
  SQ3R technique, using, 49–52,
    53, 54, 56, 57
  strategies, for critical, 65–86
  triple highlighting technique,
    using, 54–56
Rooney, A., 100
Root, 13
  Greek, 10, 14
  Latin, 10, 14
Root words, 10, 12–14, 23

S

Saki (H.H. Munro), 146–49
Scanning, 58–59
  definition of, 60
Search engine, 156
Shakespeare, W., 102
Simile, 91–97
  definition of, 103
  practice in using, 93–97
Skimming, 56–58
  definition of, 60
Smalley, S., 71

Sounded vowel, 11
Source, 85
  triangulation of, 164
Sponsor, website, 162–63
SQ3R technique, 32, 36–37, 39, 40
  definition of, 60
  as textbook reading method,
    49–52, 53, 54, 56, 57
Steinbeck, J., 115–16
Strategies
  comprehension, 27–41
  computer reading and writing,
    155–74
  critical reading, 75–85
  figurative language, 91–105
  textbook, 45–61
  vocabulary, 3–14
Suffix, 10, 12–14, 23
Syllabication, 10, 11–12, 22–23
  rules, 12
Syllables
  closed, 11
  open, 11
Synthesizing, 75–85
  fact and opinion, 76–78
  identifying author attitude, bias,
    tone, assumptions, 82–85
  identifying writer's purpose, 75–76
  validity, judging, 78–82

T

Table of contents, 46
  definition of, 60
Testimonial, 81
Textbook organizational aids, 45–48
  appendix, 46
  definition of, 60
  glossary, 46
  index, 46
  preface, 46
  table of contents, 46
Textbook strategies, 45–61
  definition of, 60
  reading methods, 48–56

skimming and scanning, 56–59
  textbook aids, using, 45–48
Thesis statement, 31
Thomas, L., 92
Thottam, J., 29
Title, as aid in comprehension,
  66–67
Tone
  definition of, 86
  identifying, 82–85
Toolbar
  formatting, 170
  Microsoft Internet Explorer, 158
  for Microsoft Word, 168
Topics
  definition of, 31, 40
  identifying, 27–30, 38
  SQ3R technique, 32
Transition words, 111, 112–13, 117
  definition of, 133
Triangulation, of sources, 164
Triple highlighting technique,
  54–56
  definition of, 60

V

Validity, 78–82
  all or nothing opinions, 80
  definition of, 85–86
  emotional appeal, 79
  of evidence, 78
  false cause, 81
  hazy generalization, 80
  name-calling, 80
  testimonial, 81
Validity, of websites
  author, 163
  content, 164
  copyright, 164
  corroboration, 164–65
  date, 163
  sponsor, 162–63
Vocabulary builders, 14

Vocabulary strategies, 3–14, 69
  context clues, 3–9
  denotation and connotation,
    21–22
  word analysis, 10–14

W

5 W and H questions, 35
Webmaster, 163
Web page, 156
Websites, evaluating, 161–66, 172
  checklist for, 166
  design and navigability, 161–62
  purpose, meeting, 161
  validity of information, 162–65
Webster's New World Dictionary, 21
Whitford, B., 36
Wiesel, E., 84
Wiley, 101
Woodbury, 35
Word analysis, 10–14
  root words, 10
  syllabication, 10

Word processing basics, 167–71,
    172
  creating document, 168–69
  editing document, 169
  formatting document, 170–71
  formatting toolbar, 170
  reference guide, 167–71
  reopening document, 170
  saving document, 169
Words
  negative, 83
  positive, 83
  transition, 111, 112–13, 117
World Wide Web, 155
  definition of, 172
Writer's purpose
  definition of, 85
  identifying, 75–76

Y

Yahoo, 161